Civil Procedure in the Czech Republic

Civil Procedure in the Czech Republic

Second Edition

Alena Macková

This book was originally published as a monograph in the International Encyclopaedia of Laws/Civil Procedure.

Founding Editor: Roger Blanpain
General Editor: Frank Hendrickx
Volume Editor: Piet Taelman

Wolters Kluwer

Published by:
Kluwer Law International B.V.
PO Box 316
2400 AH Alphen aan den Rijn
The Netherlands
E-mail: international-sales@wolterskluwer.com
Website: lrus.wolterskluwer.com

Sold and distributed in North, Central and South America by:
Wolters Kluwer Legal & Regulatory U.S.
7201 McKinney Circle
Frederick, MD 21704
United States of America
Email: customer.service@wolterskluwer.com

Sold and distributed in all other countries by:
Air Business Subscriptions
Rockwood House
Haywards Heath
West Sussex
RH16 3DH
United Kingdom
Email: international-customerservice@wolterskluwer.com

Printed on acid-free paper

ISBN 978-94-035-0945-7

e-Book: ISBN 978-94-035-0984-6
web-PDF: ISBN 978-94-035-1032-3

Printed in the United Kingdom.

The Author

Alena Macková, Doc. Dr. iur., PhD (Charles University, Prague). Associate Professor at the Civil Law Department, Law School, Charles University.
A. Macková is a member of the International Association of Procedural Law; a member of the Commission on the new procedural law of the Ministry of Justice of the Czech Republic; Member of the Board of the Academy of Justice. She is an Ombudsman of the Czech Insurance Association, an arbiter of the Czech Arbitration Court attached to the Economic Chamber of the Czech Republic and Agricultural Chamber of the Czech Republic and an arbiter of the International Arbitration Court attached to the Czech-Moravian Commodity Exchange.
Her research interests include issues such as the position and the role of judges, notaries, attorneys, the civil procedure, the role of legal professions in the protection of rights, the effectiveness of the judicial protection of rights and freedoms, alternative disputes resolution (ADR), legal aid, electronic communication, etc. She has published extensively in hereinabove mentioned areas, e.g., '*The Independence of the Judge*' (1996 – Awarded the Rector of the UK and the Rule of Law Foundation Prizes); '*The Attorneys and Their Services*' (2001-C. H. Beck); *The Civil Procedure Code* I–II, Commentary (co-author), Wolters Kluwer, 2009; *E-government Law*, Commentary (co-author), Wolters Kluwer, 2009; *The Civil Law*, I (co-author), Wolters Kluwer, 2013; *The Civil Code Commentary* I–VI. (co-author), Wolters Kluwer, 2015; *The Law on Attorneys*, (co-author), C. H. Beck, Prague 2017; *The Civil Procedure Law* Volume I–Volume II. (chief co-author, 9th ed.), Leges Prague, 2018; etc.

Author's experience includes (*inter alia*) Visiting Lectureship at the Catholic University Leuven; Democratic Institution Fellowships (Brussels); Summer Law School, SanFrancisco–Dublin Summer School in Prague – lecturership; Socrates-Erasmus + Programme tutorship, LLM Programme tutorship, visiting scholarships at the Ruprecht-Karls-University Heidelberg, Ludwig-Maximilian University Munich, University Passau, University Regensburg, Johannes Kepler University Linz, Vienna University, University Komensky Bratislava; research stay at the Court of Justice of the European Union in Luxembourg; etc.

The Author

Table of Contents

Table of Contents

List of Abbreviations

CJ	Act on Courts and Judges
Coll.	Collection of Acts and Collection of International Treaties
CPC	Civil Procedure Code
ECJ	European Court of Justice
IPLP	International Private Law and International Civil Procedure

List of Abbreviations

General Introduction

§1. General Background (The Political and Legal System of the Czech Republic)

1. The Czech Republic – as an independent state – exists since 1 January 1993 (former Czechoslovakia was divided by the formation of a contract between two representatives of the Czech and Slovak Republics). The Czech Republic is a Member State of the European Union (EU) since 4 May 2004. The Czech Republic thus fully adheres to the EU law system (EU regulations and directives and the case law of the Court of Justice of the European Union, seated in Luxembourg). In 1992, the Czech Republic signed and fully validated the European Convention on Human Rights, the compliance of which is subject to the jurisdiction of the European Court of Human Rights in Strasbourg.

2. The constitutional system of the Czech Republic consists of the Parliament (the House of Deputies and the Senate) with the legislative power, the President (the head of the Republic – selected in the direct presidential election) and the Government (both the executive bodies). The regional self-government system is fully established. The judicial system is enshrined in the constitutional system as an independent power.

3. The basic historical roots of the political, constitution and legal systems should be mentioned briefly as well. The Czechoslovak Republic (established after World War I in 1918) was one of the successors of the Austro-Hungarian Empire, which was under the Habsburg Dynasty rule. The Czech nation (besides the Slovak nation), both Slavic nations with deep historical roots and legacy, became components of the different parts of the Austro-Hungarian Monarchy – see §8 below, which is significant for its further legal development.

4. The Czechoslovak Republic was thus established on 28 October 1918 (and its leader was Prof. T. G. Masaryk as the first President of the Czechoslovak Republic) by common declaration of the Czech and Slovak nations and recognized as one of the results of the post-World War I establishment made by the Versailles Agreement.

5. The first effort of the establishment of the new republic was to rebuild basic institutions of the democratic legal system, to establish an economic system and to deal with post-war consequences, especially in the economy (like unemployment, inflation and other social problems).

6. In respect to the legal system, it should be stressed that the new republic assumed the law system of Austria due to the principle of legal continuity.

7. The milestones of Austrian legal system at this point are: first, the Civil Code (the General Civil Code of the Austria) of 1811 and the Civil Procedure Code (CPC) of 1895, as well as Code of Execution of 1896. The new republic considered this as a transitional solution, and strong effort was dedicated to prepare a new legal system with its pillars like Civil Code.

Then started another part of the existence of the Czechoslovak Republic: its occupation by Germany and establishment of the Protectorate of the Czech and Moravia, which halted all the intentions and plans (although a lot of work was done already – the draft of the new Civil Code was finished in 1937 act.).

8. After World War II (1945–1950), there was a short period of legal dualism (i.e., a different law in the Czech Lands and a different law at the Slovak lands as it was during the Austrio-Hungarian Monarchy and after the reception of its law by the new Czechoslovak Republic).

9. The main impact to the law was made by the political situation in the East and Central Europe (so-called lands behind 'iron curtains') as the result of the political division in the World after World War II.

10. The following development was not without impact on the law.

11. The Constitution of 1960 declares socialism as a base of its system with the Civil Code of 1964, Family Law of 1963, Labour Law Code of 1965, etc., as its pillars. Jurisprudence has negated and denied the distinction between private and public law, which was reflected into legal systems, and private law institutions were not supported anymore by law (no commercial obligations – no need of the commercial law). The distinction between adversary and non-adversary proceeding was denied by Civil Procedure Code of 1963 as well.

12. Another milestone in its modern history is the 'Velvet Revolution' of 1989. Within a short span, a completely new regulation was needed for all private and public law institutions (property, free enterprise, position of the judge, attorney, notary, etc.). It was made by prompt and partial amendments. The task to rebuild a legal system remains as an urgent goal.

13. A lot of legislation on the field of justice and protection of the rights was adopted since that time: No. 85/1996 Coll. on Attorneys, No. 358/1992 Coll. on Notaries, No. 6/2002 Coll. on Courts and Judges and the Civil Code (New) in 2012 (No.89/2012 Coll., effective from 1 January 2014).

§2. Delimitation of the Subject Matter

I. Definition of the Term 'Civil Procedure'

14. The notion and the conception of the civil procedure are stipulated in the private law, resp. in its relation to the procedural law. Article 12 of the Civil Code stipulates the right to ask for the protection of the rights. The access to the court is guaranteed by the Constitution and the Charter of the Fundamental Rights and Freedoms. In compliance with Article 13 of CC, this protection of the rights has to be predictable (if there is a judgment different from previous, it has to be fully reasoned). Article 1 of the CPC (in compliance with Article 36 of the Charter of the Fundamental Rights and Freedoms) declares its goal: to provide a fair protection of the rights to everybody. With regard to jurisprudence thus follows:

(1) the civil procedure is the procedure before the court (or other entitled body – e.g., arbiter);
(2) the goal of the civil procedure is to protect (private law) rights;
(3) the relationship between the subjects of the procedure (the court, the parties, the witness, the expert and any others) during the proceedings has special procedural nature with special rights and duties arising (the contradictory principle, the right to be present at the hearing, etc.);
(4) the protection of the rights provided by the civil procedure is thus fully rendered if the judgment is issued (the rights and duties are adjusted) and – when the judgment is not respected – if it is enforced. However, apart from these two kinds of proceedings (adjudication and enforcement), there are other goals of the civil procedure arising from the private law, which have to be fulfilled.

II. Distinction with Other Types of Procedure

15. The court with general jurisdiction provides the protection of the rights to the rights arising from the private law. Besides, a criminal procedure is stipulated into a Code of Criminal Procedure and the review of the administrative authorities by the courts (administrative judiciary) is stipulated in the Code on Administrative Judiciary (No. 150/2002 Coll.).

16. Particular attention needs to be given to administrative judiciary in the Czech Republic, which carries out an independent judicial review of administrative decisions. Once again, to fully appreciate the issue, we need to look back into history. Like the former Austro-Hungarian Empire, the Czechoslovak Republic had a very progressive administrative judiciary represented by the Supreme Administrative Court established according to the Austrian model. The Supreme Administrative Court successfully operated until 1950. It was abolished after 1950. It was not abolished merely due to the fact that organizational reform was needed at that time as the Supreme Administrative Court, as the only court of its kind, was overloaded. The main reason for its abolishment was an ideological opposition to the existence of an independent judicial review of the administration. Such judicial review was in direct contradiction with the prevailing ideology which was later incorporated in the Constitution of the Czechoslovak Socialist Republic.

17. The administrative judiciary ceased to exist for forty years, with the exception of a handful of public law relations in connection with which courts carried out the review as a part of civil procedure (only one area, the old-age pension and social security systems, was of some practical significance). The lack of a general administrative judiciary was considered to be one of the shortcomings in the development towards democracy after 1989. That is why administrative judiciary was reintroduced speedily (as early as in 1992) on the basis of the so-called general clause which allowed for the judicial review of administrative decisions unless provided otherwise by the law. The courts do so in the civil proceedings.

18. This is not to say that the Czech Republic gave up on the idea of the independent administrative judiciary. In fact, on 1 January 2003, the Code of Judicial Administrative Procedure came into effect establishing the Supreme Administrative Court and setting forth the rules of administrative proceedings. The Code of Judicial Administrative Procedure covers all aspects of administrative judiciary; however, it maintains subsidiary application of the Code of Civil Procedure. In addition, civil judiciary review of administrative decisions is also maintained in some matters. As a result, many experts, also citing theoretical reasons, have doubts about whether administrative judiciary has truly become an independent procedure or whether it continues to be a part – albeit specialized – of the civil procedure. Potential jurisdictional conflicts between civil and administrative procedure are addressed by a specialized bench of judges appointed in parity from among judges of the Supreme Court and the Supreme Administrative Court.

19. The proper rendering of the protection of rights is observed by the Constitutional Court. It can examine either (1) general (abstract) constitutionality of the act (to control the adopted laws – abstract control) or (2) individual (concrete) constitutionality of the acts (the judgment of the court or any other public authority body issued in individual case – concrete control) and declare if there is the conformity of the act with the constitutional demands like with the right to fair trial under Article 36 of the Charter of the Fundamental Rights and Freedoms.

20. Anyone can ask the Constitutional Court to review the judgment of the court in particular case under conditions stipulated (constitutional complaint is admissible only if all the legal remedies have been used before). The applicant must be represented by the attorney, and he/she declares the violation of his/her constitutional rights or freedom by the court.

III. Are There Separate Court Systems and Rules of Procedure?

21. There is a single court system in the Czech Republic (and consisting of four elements). These so-called courts of general jurisdiction are courts with exclusive jurisdiction in both civil and criminal matters. The system includes district courts (of which there are eighty-six), regional courts (eight), High Courts (two) and the Supreme Court of the Czech Republic. The High Courts are located in Prague and Olomouc, whereas the Supreme Court sits in Brno (*see* www.nsoud.cz). Due to eco nomic rather than organizational reasons, the 2003 legislation created an asymmet rical model in the area of administrative judiciary. The asymmetry means that the supreme body of administrative judiciary is the Supreme Administrative Court sea ted in Brno, but the lower-instance courts were not established. Specialized benches of judges at regional courts of general jurisdiction hear administrative cases. They serve as courts of first instance. The Supreme Administrative Court then reviews cas sation complaints against decisions of the specialized benches or judges.

The Constitutional Court stands completely outside the described court system. Rules of procedure will be mentioned bellow.

§3. Sources of Civil Procedure Law

22. The basic source of the civil procedure is the Constitution of the Czech Republic (Constitutional Act No. 1/1993 of the Collection of Laws – hereinafter 'Coll.') together with the Charter of Fundamental Rights and Freedoms (Act No. 2/1993 Coll.) which forms an inherent part of the Czech constitutional order. In Part IV, the Constitution covers the 'Judiciary' and sets forth basic principles of judicial proceedings and the protection of the rights. Further, Article 10 of the Constitution stipulates that ratified international treaties are a part of the legal order and prevail over domestic laws. This is extremely significant for court proceedings.

The Bill (Charter) of Fundamental Rights and Freedoms provides, in its Part Five, for the 'right to court or other legal protection' (Article 36 and following).

23. The source of the civil procedure law are the Code of Civil Procedure (Act No. 99/1963 Coll. as amended), the Act No. 292/2013 Coll. on the Non-adversary Proceeding, the Act on Arbitration and Enforcement of Arbitration Awards (Act No. 216/1994 Coll.as amended), Act No. 182/2006 Coll. on the Insolvency Proceedings, as amended, and the Code of Judicial Administrative Procedure (Act No. 150/2002 Coll. as amended).

In the area of execution of judgments, there is, in addition to the Code of Civil Procedure which contains a general regulation and rules on enforcement of judgments, the Code on Executors and Rules of Execution (Act No. 120/2001 Coll. as amended).

24. As regards the organization of the court system and the role of judges as well as other officers of the judiciary, it is covered by the Act on Courts and Judges (Act No. 6/2002 Coll.), the Attorney's Act (Act No. 85/1996 Coll.), Notarial Rules (Act No. 358/1992 Coll.) and the Act on Judicial Officers (Act No. 189/1994 Coll.).

25. Other important pieces of legislation covering the civil procedure are the Act on Court Experts and Interpreters (Act No. 36/1967 Coll.), the proposal of the new regulation on Experts was submitted to the Parliament in 2018, the Act on Court

Fees (Act No. 549/1991 Coll.) and the secondary legislation – for instance, the rules of proceedings for courts, the regulation on fees and cost reimbursements for attorneys and lawyers and others.

The legal regulation of the Civil Procedure in the Czech Republic is a written law.

26. However, it is also the case law of the Constitutional Court of the Czech Republic which has, especially recently, contributed significantly to the formation of the civil procedure with relevant impact. In addition to rulings on individual constitutional complaints (concrete control of its constitutionality), the Constitutional Court may also revoke Acts or their parts in cases where these are found to be in contradiction with the constitutional order (abstract control of the constitutionality). The Constitutional Court revoked several provisions of the Code of Civil Procedure in this manner.

Although not considered as a formal source of law, the findings of the Constitutional Court regarding individual complaints as well as the case law of the Supreme Court and the Supreme Administrative Court help create modern civil procedure of a democratic society.

The case law of the Supreme Court forms (by the unification of the case law) the practice of the Czech Court not being a formal source of the law contrary the written law.

§4. General Features of the Administration of Justice in Civil Matters

I. Characteristics of the Procedure

27. The Constitution of the Czech Republic stipulates that the justice is rendered by independent courts which do so in the name of the Republic (public power performance). Furthermore, the Constitution states that the courts are organized in a system of courts with general power – civil law and criminal law matters (as described above – consisting of four elements – Supreme Court, High Courts, regional courts and district courts). No other (special) courts can exist than those established through the Constitution.

In rendering the protection of rights, the courts and judges are independent. Their independence must not be interfered with in any manner. The independence of the judiciary and the judges is guaranteed by various legal remedies and institutions, e.g., the lifetime appointment by the President of the Republic (a judge may be recalled only on the basis of disciplinary proceedings carried out by the independent judge) or the system of the liability of the judge.

28. The Constitution further stipulates that in decision-making, the judges are bound by law and international treaties that are part of the legal order only. If a court considers that an applicable law is in conflict with the constitutional order, it passes the matter onto the Constitutional Court. Courts themselves may not decide on the unconstitutionality of a law; however, they may rule on the legality of a secondary legislation (for instance, a regulation), i.e., on its conformity or conflict with law, and may draw conclusions for their rulings.

29. In addition, the Constitution defines the roles of judiciary generally: the courts are to protect rights of the individuals in a manner prescribed by law. The Constitution grounds certain general principles of the proceedings: all parties are equal before the court (the principle of equality of the parties), the proceedings before the court (the courts hearing) are oral (the proceedings without hearing is admitted as an exception in particular proceedings or with the consent of the parties) and public, except for some exemptions given by law and the judgment is always rendered publicly (the principle of oral and public hearing).

30. Civil procedure is principally based on a two-instance procedure: in the first instance proceedings, district courts rule most often, and in the second (appellate) instance, regional courts hear the case and review the judgment issued by an instance court. In some matters prescribed by law, regional courts serve as first instance courts, whereas the High Courts hear the appeals (will review the judgment of the Regional Court as a court of the first instance) as courts of second instance. This irregularity pertains to certain special matters which otherwise fall under the full jurisdiction of the civil courts (like Mergers and Acquisitions disputes or intellectual property disputes).

31. Appeals are permissible in all civil matters with a few exceptions: claims under Czech Koruna (CZK) 10,000, i.e., roughly Euro (EUR) 380 (bagatelle matter), may not be subject to appeal. In addition to the appeal, there are other extraordinary remedies, namely review (as a means of cassation) to the Supreme Court of the Czech Republic, renewal of the process (retrial) and action for nullity (nullity plea).

Usually, a single judge decides at the first instance. Only in labour matters, rulings are handed down by a bench consisting of the presiding judge and two lay judges. In the second instance, the appeal, a three-member bench comprised of judges renders the decision.

32. One of the characteristic features of the Czech civil procedure (its adjudication part) is the principle difference between the adversary procedure (for which the principle of disposition, the contradictory and concentration principles are typical) and non-adversary proceedings (in which the principle of officiality, the inquisitorial principle and principle of unity of the litigation are applied). This differentiation is reflected in the current law (there is a special regulation of the non-adversary proceeding in the Act No. 292/2013 Coll. as amended).

33. To make civil procedure and the protection of the rights speedy and more effective in general, some amendments of the CPC were adopted in the last few years. This, however, seems to be a permanent task, such as a default judgment, concentrated adversary proceedings (with time limits for the parties under procedurals sanctions), electronic communication, different options of summary proceedings, including an issuance of payment order or electronic payment order or non-oral proceedings as a subject to the consent of the parties and others. These are all procedural means of the adversary procedure that were not to be found in the original Code of Civil Procedure of 1963. The use of these procedural means is limited to adversary procedure, and they are expressly banned in the non-adversary procedure. The biggest difference which is given by the very nature of the adversary versus non-adversary procedure exists with respect to procedural liability of the parties for the establishment of facts of the claim and presentation of the evidence. Briefly, this procedural responsibility rests with the parties in the adversary proceedings (burden of the statement of fact and burden of proof), but not in non-adversary proceedings, whose goal and the relation to the civil law is different.

34. Civil procedure is principally an adversary procedure. What falls among non-adversary matters is determined by the lawmaker. Thus, in the Czech Republic not only traditional matters, such as matters of personal status (including divorce), protection of minors and protection of missing persons, but also matters such as, the financial market and the proceedings on inheritance are considered to be non-adversary. The law has it that such matters should be considered non-adversary which, due to a need to protect a weaker party or public interest, are not desired to be fully in the hands of the parties and out of the control of the judge. As a rule, non-adversary proceedings may be initiated ex officio.

35. This differentiation deepens over time and has an impact on the role of the judge and the parties in the proceedings. Consequently, the differentiation between the adversary and non-adversary procedure concerns the factual, not the legal aspects of the matter, because the legal qualification is in many cases a matter for the court. The court is to apply the law. The principle *iura novit curia* ('the court knows the law') applies in Czech civil procedure in general. That means that in the adversary process, where the contradictory principle applies, it is the liability of the parties to establish facts, whereas in the non-adversary process, in which the inquisitorial principle prevails over the discovery, the facts have to be found out by the court in coordination with the parties. As a result, the judge may admit evidence other than that proposed by the parties in exceptional circumstances.

36. Furthermore, the adversary principle in civil procedure is softened by the fact that there is no mandatory requirement for legal representation in the civil proceedings. The only exception to this is extraordinary appellate review before the Supreme Court. Otherwise, parties in both adversary and non-adversary proceedings may represent themselves without attorneys. The only requirement is their procedural capacity (which equals their legal capacity). This applies equally to appellate procedure. Parties always have the option to be represented by an attorney.

37. The role of the judge in the Czech justice system is rendered more difficult as he/she has to cope with lay views on the law. The law obliges the judges to instruct parties in their procedural (only) rights and obligations. Thus, the theoretical adversary principle is undoubtedly undermined.

It should be added that the same applies to the administrative judiciary proceedings. However, in criminal proceedings (starting with offences of specified seriousness) and in the proceedings before the Constitutional Court, legal representation is mandatory.

II. Fundamental Guarantees

38. The Czech civil procedure gives full recognition to the right to a fair trial as one of the fundamental human rights under Article 6 of the European Convention on Human Rights. The Czech Republic is fully bound by this Convention (1992) and strives to adhere to it. Additionally, the right to a fair trial is guaranteed by the Constitution of the Czech Republic and by the Charter of Fundamental Rights and Freedoms (Article 36 of which guarantees the right to a fair trial with all its requisites).

In addition to the above-mentioned provisions of the Constitution regarding the independence and impartiality of the judiciary, the equality before the court and the principle of oral proceedings, it is the Bill/Charter of Fundamental Rights and Freedoms (hereinafter 'Bill/Charter') which is an integral component of the constitutional order of the Czech Republic and which serves as a guarantee of individual aspects of the right to fair trial.

39. In Part V of the Bill 'Right to Judicial and Other Legal Protection' ('Everyone has the right to seek protection of his rights from an independent and impartial court'), the general right to legal action (claim) is defined with a special emphasis on the right to review of the public administration's decisions and on the liability of State for unlawful decisions or wrongful performance of the power. Furthermore, the Bill/Charter stipulates, *inter alia*, those rights and principles: equality before the court, right to legal aid and right to translation for those who do not have a command of the Czech language, etc.

40. Furthermore, it also stipulates that no one has to be removed from the jurisdiction of the legal judge (right to a legal judge). Finally, the Bill/Charter guarantees that everyone has the right to public hearing of his/her matter, without undue delays, in his/her presence, and that everyone has the right to speak to the evidence presented.

41. Being elements of the right to fair trial, all of the above constitutional rights are under the observation and control of the Constitutional Court of the Czech Republic, and any infringement of those rights gives grounds for a constitutional complaint (*see* above).

42. The relevant laws (namely the procedural codes, i.e., Code of Civil Procedure, Code of Criminal Procedure and the Code of Judicial Administrative Procedure) gradually eliminate all such provisions which may be found in conflict with these principles, albeit in detail and partially. At the same time, such legal measures are adopted which enhance adherence to all elements of the right to fair process.

43. As far as the delays in the proceedings are concerned, there are effective remedies for the parties in the Czech legal system (*see* Article 174a of the Act on Courts and Judges, stipulating the special claim to the higher (superordinate) court, by which the party can ask to order the lower court to make a procedural movement in the proceeding, when delay is made by this court), and the courts have procedural tools against the delays caused by the parties as well.

Part I. Judicial Organization

Chapter 1. The Courts and the Bar

§1. The Courts and Their Members

I. Structure of the Court System

The System of the Courts and the Jurisdiction of the Courts are defined in the Constitution of the Czech Republic ('Ústava České republiky'/Act No. 1/1993 Coll. as amended). The Czech Courts System is composed of four elements: Supreme Court, High Courts, regional courts and district courts. The law (Act 6/2002 Coll. as amended) defines titles, seats and districts of the courts in the Czech Republic.

44. Alongside this system of courts with general jurisdiction, there exists the Constitutional Court. The Constitutional Court implements the constitutional judiciary, i.e., the constitutional control in the Czech legal system. The administrative judiciary is implemented by the Supreme Administrative Court as the court of cassation and by the regional courts (by the specialized benches).

45. The district Courts are the lowest level in the Czech Judiciary system. The district courts have jurisdiction to decide cases, which are not in the jurisdiction of the regional courts (Article 9 section 2 of CPC). There are eighty-six district courts in the Czech Republic. The law (Act No. 6/2002 Coll. on Courts and Judges) defines the titles, seats and districts of these courts.

The regional courts handle and decide the cases either as the courts of the first instance or as the courts of appeal (second instance).

District and regional courts traditionally allocate caseload and specific cases according to their specializations. This has been proved popular because the caseload becomes more equitable between the courts and there is a greater guarantee that experienced judges are allocated for more difficult cases. The divisions between the agendas of the two levels of the judiciary system provide a benefit because it assures a degree of unification in the decisions of the courts.

46. For example, the regional courts have the competence to decide (as the courts of the first instance) cases dealing with issues of the corporations, intellectual property disputes and other strictly defined cases, which are rendered serious and complex either from a legal angle or by their subject matter (*see* Article 9 section 2 of CPC).

The regional courts keep the public registries and make decisions in cases dealing with it (commercial register, the register of non-profit entities and foundations, cooperations, the register of the ownership of apartment units): cases on the legal status of these subjects; disputes dealing with the particularities of these subjects (e.g., disputes between the founders and companies); cases dealing with economic competition; cases dealing with securities (public markets securities), bankruptcy and solutions of disputes arising from bankruptcy proceedings; cases dealing with the capital markets' issues; cases focused on the validity of contracts on the establishment of a European Company (which has been previously adopted by a board of directors), etc.

The law (Act 6/2002 Coll. as amended) defines titles, seats and districts of the Courts in the Czech Republic.

The High Courts are the courts of appeal. The High Courts hear cases which were decided in the first instance by the regional courts.

There are two High Courts in the Czech Republic (the title, seats and districts are defined by the Act 6/2002 Coll. on Courts and Judges, as amended).

47. The Constitution considers the Supreme Court to be the highest body of judicial power with the exception of matters concerning the Constitutional Court or the Supreme Administrative Court. The Supreme Court consists of a presiding judge, his/her deputy and other judges. According to the Article 62 f) of the Constitution, the presiding judge and his/her deputy are appointed by the President of the Czech Republic. The Supreme Court is competent to decide on extraordinary appeal, i.e., extraordinary post-trial remedies, against decisions of Regional and High Courts in its capacity as an appellate court.

48. The power of the Supreme Court is to unify the decision-making of the Czech Courts (its decisions are published – *see* www.nsoud.cz). Supreme Court makes decisions on legal remedies (extraordinary appeal) against judgments of the courts of appeal (which might be either Regional or High Courts), decisions on the recognition and enforcement of judgments issued by foreign courts for the territory of the Czech Republic: whether it concerns the law or an international treaty. To unify the decision-making of the Czech Courts, the Supreme Court may adopt an approach to the interpretation of the law (persisting from previous legal system). This approach is based on analysis of the judgments of the courts on the particular matters.

49. The Supreme Administrative Court has its power in administrative judiciary to decide on cassation against the judgments of the Regional Court adopted by its specialized benches (other cases are determined by the Act No. 150/2005 Coll. Code of Administrative Judiciary). The Supreme Administrative Court has, like the Supreme Court, the main role to unify the decision-making of the administrative courts.

II. Administration of the Courts

50. The courts of the Czech Republic are administrated by the system of the State administration. The State court administration is supplemented by elements of self-government. The State court administration has a long tradition in the Czech Republic.

The authorities for the administration of the courts are the presidents of the courts (vice presidents of the courts) and the central administration of the courts. The latter is entrusted to the Ministry of Justice of the Czech. The Ministry of Justice oversees other activities and competencies: e.g., to control the public prosecution, to write the drafts for new legislation, to administrate the prisons, to provide the legal cooperation in the international relations with foreign countries, etc.

The Ministry of Justice of the Czech Republic, within the administration of the courts, secures the proper operation of the courts by the provision of a sufficient number of judges and other employees of the courts, by financing of the courts and providing for the material requirements to operate the courts. The Ministry of Justice has the power to control the activities of the presidents of the District, Regional and High Courts as far as the property of the State is concerned. The law (sections 124 and following of Law No. 6/2002 Coll. on Courts and Judges) determines the role of the presidents of the courts as overseers of the State court's administration.

The president of each court appoints the director of court administration. The role of the director of court administration as an employee of the court is to secure the operation of the court concerned. The president of the court's responsibility is to provide for the proper administration regardless of the competencies of the director of the court administration.

The council of judges is a self-governmental body that administers the Czech courts and advises the president of the court in certain areas (as its advisory board). Councils of judges are established at all courts in the Czech Republic (except in small district courts with less than ten judges). The council of the judges is elected by judges who are members of certain courts. An assembly of all the judges elects the members of the council of judges by secret ballot in an equal vote. The president of the council of the judges is elected on the first session of the elected council of judges.

The council of the judges discusses the nominee for the function of president of the court and his deputy, decide about the judges who should work at the court, decides about the judges who should leave the court for advancement in their career and discuss about the judge who should be appointed as a presiding judge of the benches of the court. The councils of the judges discuss the schedule of work for the courts and recommend to the president of the court the members of the special bench, which controls the decision-making of the judges of the court. There is a limited term for a decision of the council of judges by the law in certain matters. If there is no decision rendered by the council of judges during the time limit, it is assumed that it agrees with the proposals of the president of the court. The council of judges can adopt its decisions, when more than half of its members are present at its sessions and the decision is adopted or when it is agreed on by the more than half of the present members of the council. The councils of judges are institutions created for the administration of the court.[1]

III. The Appointment of the Judges

51. The legal status of a judge is determined by the Constitution and by law and other regulations. The nominee has to go through the preparatory period as a trainee. The Ministry of Justice pursues the selection and the entrance of the trainees.

The successful trainee is chosen in a selection procedure organized by the Academy of Justice (see www.jacz.cz), which is announced by the president of the Reg ional Court or Ministry of Justice. The trainee is then given a contract for a forty -month period at the court.

The preparatory service period focuses on intensifying the special legal knowledge of the trainee, either in procedural or substantive law, the development of the ability to apply legal regulations to concrete situations, to acquire knowledge in particular agendas of the courts, to adopt the procedural habits needed for the work of judge and to study the ethical limits of the functions of a judge.

Every trainee has a tutor during the preparatory service period. The president of the Regional Court appoints the tutors, and they are selected from experienced judges, who are able to bring up the trainees. The tutor is obliged to make a detailed personal file for each trainee where all data are registered about their preparatory service (the place, the time, the content and the evaluation of the preparatory service). The trainee is entitled to comment on the registered data in his/her personal file.

During the preparatory service period, the trainee can spend some practice at another court, State attorney's office, in the office of an attorney or in the notary's office, police or public administration authority. The course of the preparatory service period also consists of lectures and seminars. The lectures and seminars are organized by the Academy of Justice. These programmes start with a special course, which is prepared for the first six months of the preparatory service period.

The preparatory service period takes thirty-six months and is finished by an exam. The special exam for judges takes place before a commission, which is appointed by the Minister of Justice. The commission consists of five members (judges, employees of the Ministry of Justice, and academics and practitioners). The exam has two parts: oral and written. The written part of the exam consists of drafting a judgment in criminal law, civil law and an administrative judiciary judgment in the case, which are selected by lot.

The oral part of the exam consists of constitutional law and judiciary law, civil law, civil procedural law, labour law, social security law, family law, criminal law

1. A. Macková, *Nezávislost soudc* (*The Independence of the Judge*) 3rd edn. (UK Praha, 1998), p. 53; A. Winterová, A. Macková et al., *Civilní právo procesní* (*The Civil Procedure*) 9th edn. (Praha, 2018).

and criminal procedural law, commercial law, administrative judiciary and administrative law and other regulations (i.e., on notaries and executors) and EU law. A good understanding of the sources of international public law is expected. The exam can be repeated once.

The President of the Republic appoints judges. The requirements for the appointment are Czech citizenship, an unblemished character, a minimum age of 30 years on the day of appointment and agreement for the appointment to a concrete court. The experience and moral quality of the nominee should guarantee their proper performance of the function as a judge. The nominee has to have a full legal education in a master of law programme at an accredited law school in the Czech Republic. After the appointment, the judge has to take a vow at the hands of the President of the Czech Republic.

The judges are appointed for life tenure. The law strictly determines the reasons for expiration of their term. The judge can resign his function. Their term will expire when they turn 70 years old. Their term expires also if the judge is sentenced for a wilful crime or if the judge is sentenced to prison for a negligent crime. The term of the judge will expire in other cases also (e.g., the loss of legal capacity of the judge, the loss of citizenship, the death of the judge/the declaration of the death of the judge and the dismissal of the judge because of a disciplinary offence).

52. The judge and the lay judge are positions of public concern. A judge has a number of legal duties and limitations. The judges are independent, and their independence and impartiality are guaranteed. Judges have to make decisions according to their conscience and are bound by law. Judicial power is founded upon democratic principles of the independence and impartiality of courts and judges.

The relevant duty of Czech judges is to make decisions in a reasonable/adequate time limit without delays, impartiality, fair and based upon the facts, which are investigated legally.

The role of a judge brings certain limitations to his/her private life also (dignity in private life has to be followed).

53. There are lay judges in the Czech Judiciary system. Their role is to make decisions on the benches with professional judges (Article 94 section 2 of the Constitution). The lay judges are members of the benches of the courts of first instance. In civil litigation, only labour law cases are decided by such mixed court benches (Article 36 of CPC). The value of their vote is equivalent to the vote of the professional judge. A majority of votes determine the decision and every member of the bench is obliged to vote.

The sequence of voting is strictly determined to avoid influences on the bench: the lay judges have to vote before the professional judges and the younger judges have to vote before the older judges. The presiding judge (chief of the bench) votes the last. The lay judges are not obliged to be educated in law and to pass an exam. The other conditions for their role are the same as for a nominee for the function of a professional judge.

The local assemblies of the district are where the lay judges of a certain court stand for election. There is a condition that the nominee has to work or to have domicile in the district in which they stand. After the election, it is a duty to take a vow at the hands of the president of the court to which they were elected.

There is a legal regulation concerning liability (liability for torts, criminal and disciplinary liability) for judges in the Czech Republic. There is no direct judge's liability for torts. If there is damage caused by a judgment, a judge will not be liable, and he/she is not obliged to compensate. The State is liable to compensate for damages caused by judgments. This procedure is regulated in a special law on liability of the State for damages and irregular performance of the public power (Law No. 82/1998 Coll. as amended).

The judge will be punished for every crime, but if there is a connection between the crime and the function of the judge, the judge can be punished or arrested only with the permission of the President of the Republic. If there is punishment for a judge, the Ministry of Justice (or the local assembly and the president of the court in the case that a lay judge is punished) has to be informed.

A disciplinary liability consists of the punishment for a wilful offence against the duties of the judges or behaviour against the independent, impartial and fair decision-making of the courts or against the dignity of the role of the judge.

The disciplinary procedure is held before the special benches of the Supreme Administrative Court (*see* www.nsoud.cz). The same applies if there is an offence in the personal life of a judge.[2]

---

2. A. Macková, *Nezávislost soudc* (*The Independence of the Judge*) 3rd edn. (UK Praha, 1998).

Chapter 2. The Bar

§1. Exercise of the Legal Profession

I. Conditions for Admission

54. The professions of attorneys, notaries and executors are regulated in the legal system of the Czech Republic in the Justice system as the private rights protection is concerned. Their legal positions and roles are different. One person cannot be an attorney and a notary or an executor at the same time, because these professions are separated.

The exclusive professional organization that provides for the provision of legal services in the Czech Republic is the Bar. There are about 14,000 enrolled attorneys in the Czech Republic at present. Their legal services can include representation in litigation before the different public authorities, the defence (counsel) of the perpetrator of a crime, legal consultations, the writing of different kinds of documents, legal analyses and other types of legal services, if it is provided permanently and for a fee. This profession is incorporated in the legal system by law. The State – by the adoption such a regulation – fulfils a duty to its citizens to ensure the right to legal aid (following Article 36 of the Charter of the Rights and Freedoms, which declares the right to fair trial, including the right to legal aid). The performance of the advocacy is in the public interest which is relevant for the special limitations of the profession. In its complexity, the limitations guarantee the quality and accessibility of legal services for everyone who wants to use their services. The complex rights, duties and privileges, which the Bar has in the legal system, assure that it can provide complex services in the legal system of the State. The Bar is not replaceable, and no other legal profession can substitute it, even if it is entitled to provide legal services.

The law strictly determines the conditions upon which nominees are allowed to enrol in the Bar. The nominee has to have full legal capacity, to be fully educated in law in a master of law programme and to have practised as a trainee for a minimum of three years while successfully passing the exam for attorneys. The nominee should be of an unblemished character and, at the time of enrolment, cannot be the subject of any disciplinary measure of the Bar. The taking of the vow at the hands of the president of the Czech Bar is a necessary condition for enrolment, as well.

Part III of the Czech law on Attorneys determines conditions on which lawyers from other EU Member States are allowed to perform advocacy in the Czech Republic (as seated European Lawyer or visiting European Lawyer). Attorneys from other countries (non-EU) must pass a special exam before they are allowed to provide legal services (in the field of homeland law and international law).

Determining the conditions for enrolment is relevant for the open nature of the profession, because it assures that the Bar remains an open institution. There are no other conditions for membership in the Bar except conditions determined by law for the enrolment in the Bar. A negative enrolment decision by the Bar can be reviewed by an administrative court upon the applicant's request, which determines its legality and conformity with the law.

The performance of the advocacy is governed by many factors. A primary duty that serves for the protection of clients is the examination of the education of attorneys, the duty to maintain secrecy and their direct personal liability. The attorney has to be competent and qualified, which is guaranteed by a system of training and examination. The liability for torts of an individual attorney is personal and unlimited. Attorneys have a duty to enter into a contract that provides insurance to ensure that the client is protected in the case of the insolvency of an attorney. The attorney must maintain the secrecy (which covers all the information gained during providing legal services). Some exemptions are stipulated by law (e.g., the struggle against money laundering). Apart from the law on attorneys, their rights and duties are stipulated in the Code of conduct and competitions rules and Code of conduct of the Council of the Bars and Law Societies of Europe (CCBE) (*see* www.cak.cz and ccbe.org). The following of those rules is under disciplinary commission of the profession and may give rise to penalties.

55. In a traditional classical European sense, the profession of the notary is deeply and profoundly rooted in the Czech legal system. The traditions of the profession were discontinued in 1949 and changed its nature completely; it became active as a public office. From 1989, the role of a Czech notary began to return to its pre-1949 status. This procedure was finalized on 1 January 1993, when the law on notaries came in to force (Act No. 358/1992 Coll. Notarial Rules, as amended). The notary is a natural person, who is entitled by the State to perform the public power in the notarial office (the office of the notary). The office of the notary determines a special notaries' competence (power) and oversees the activities of notaries, which are laid out in the law.

56. There are more than 400 notaries in the Czech Republic at present. A notary has some capabilities that are duplicated by other government officials, including the ability to confirm signatures or to legalize documents (in the system of e-government there are 'the Czech-points' – *see* www.czech-point.cz).

The role of a notary is to prevent disputes and to support legal certainty by providing binding verification (the confirmation of signature and the legalization of documents) and inscribing documents in the public record (public-faith documents). Such documents, written by a notary, can be used in litigation as evidence with higher probative value. A special type of notarial deed may be used as a title for enforcement directly without previous litigation (notarial deed with enforcement clause) or as a European execution title. Beside the notary's typical activity, notaries in the Czech Republic are also active as court commissioners in litigation regarding heritage and may act as a personal property representative, accepting and holding deposits for the sale or purchase of the property. The notary can also provide limited legal services. The services of a notary are fee-based. The fee for a typical notary's activities is determined in the notary's scale of fees (ordinance of Ministry of Justice No. 196/2001 Coll. as amended). If a notary provides her/his client legal services, the fee is determined by the same rules which apply in the same sense between an attorney and his/her client.

The number of notaries is limited (the *numerus clausus* principle) and is determined by the State. The Minister of Justice determines the number of notaries for each district court on the opinion of the Chamber of Notaries of the Czech Republic. The purpose of this system is to make the notary's services accessible throughout the Czech Republic for everyone. If there is an available office of a notary, the Chamber of the Notaries of the Czech Republic announces the selection procedure for everyone who meets the conditions determined by the law. Everyone legally capable, with full legal education in a master of law programme, unblemished character, having undergone years of practice and having passed a special exam can be appointed by Minister of Justice. The position is earned through employment at a notary's office. A trainee notary is entrusted with power in some areas, i.e., the confirmation of a signature or verification of documents. After the trainee successfully passes the exam, he/she becomes a notary's nominee. A notary's nominee is entitled to perform some other actions of the profession. When there is an available (free or new) notarial office, the tender is renowned and organized by the Chamber of Notaries, and the winning notarial nominee is entitled by the Minister of Justice to the notarial office.

The profession of a notary is organized on the principle of self-government, with some State regulation and supervision. This self-government is overseen by chambers of notaries, established on a regional basis at every Regional Court and by the Chamber of Notaries of the Czech Republic. Regional notaries' chambers govern professional activities inside the profession, and the Chamber of Notaries of the Czech Republic oversees functions outside the profession. The Chamber of Notaries of the Czech Republic also regulates some functions inside the profession (the organization and announcement of the selection procedure for an available office of notary, the organization of exams and the organization of advanced education for notaries). The regional chambers of notaries include all notaries, who are residents in the region and membership is obligatory. The Chamber of Notaries of the Czech Republic is the legal entity to which all the regional notaries' chambers are associated. The authorities of the Chamber of Notaries of the Czech Republic are the assembly (the supreme body), the praesidium (executive and operative body), the president (statutory body), the auditing commission (control body) and the disciplinary commission. The Chamber of Notaries of the Czech Republic operates the register of testaments (and other documents on heritage) and register of liens, register of living will and the register of the document on the property of the spouses.

57. The profession of *(court) executor* has to be differentiated from the position of executor, who works as an employee of the court. Creditors have a choice to use either the legal regime, in which an executor is active, or the legal regime of the court's execution. The executor operates for fees, which are derived from debt incurred by the judgments. The executor has wide power to ascertain information on property owned by a debtor from third parties. The court, on the contrary, assumes that the creditor has the necessary information on the property of the debtor. The debtor is capable of choosing a way to address a debt.

An executor's sole and legal status is similar to that of a notary. An executor is a natural person who is entitled to perform a public office and its power. Similar to the position of a notary, an executor is appointed to his or her office by the Minister of Justice of the Czech Republic after a success in the selection procedure for a vacant office of the executor. The Chamber of Executors of the Czech Republic organizes the selection procedure. The nominee has to have a legal capacity, have a full legal education in a master of law programme, have unblemished character, have a minimum of three years of practice as a trainee and have successfully passed a special exam.

An executor performs execution: the enforcement of judgments and other court orders (in some cases like family law matters, it is forbidden for executors to perform it, and such a judgment can be enforced just by the Court). An executor is also entitled to provide legal services to creditors and debtors, to draft special executor's documents (public-faith documents), to deliver the documents of the courts and to accept deposits and perform auctions. The activities of executors are fee-based, and these fees are determined by an ordinance of Ministry of Justice (No. 330/2001 Coll. as amended).

58. The exclusive profession entitled to provide legal services in the Czech Republic is the Bar. There are about 14,000 enrolled attorneys in the Czech Republic at present. The essential role of the Bar is to provide legal services. Legal services consist of the representation in litigation before the courts and other legal arenas, defence in criminal prosecution, legal consultation, drafting of legal documents, legal analysis and other services, provided permanently and fee-based. This profession is rooted in the legal system by law. It is the task of the State to assure the right of legal aid for everyone. The proper performance of the legal profession is in the interests of the public. The public interest governs the legal profession. Inherit is the guarantee of quality and the accessibility of the services of the Bar for everyone who needs or wants to use it. The complex rights and duties and privileges which the Bar has is a reflection of the duty of the Bar to provide the legal services in all matters. The Bar is irreplaceable in this role in the legal system, and no other profession, even entitled to provide legal services, can replace the Bar. There are conditions for the enrolment to the Bar determined strictly by the law: full legal capacity, legal education in a master of law programme, unblemished character, three years of practice as a trainee, no disciplinary measures, an exam and a vow at the hands of the president of the Bar. The determination of the legal conditions for enrolment is extremely relevant for the profession in order to be an open institution. The Bar is prevented to discourage (restrain) enrolment. Access to the profession is not limited except by the above-mentioned conditions. If there is an illegal refusal of an applicant, he/she is entitled to ask the administrative court to review the practices of the Bar.[3]

Lawyers from the other Member States of EU can provide legal services in the Czech Republic under conditions of Part III of the Law on Attorneys, which fully reflects the EU Directives (No. 77/249, No. 89/48 and No. 98/5).

---

3. A. Macková, *Právní pomoc advokát u a její dostupnost* (*Attorneys and Their Services*) (C.H. Beck, 2001); P. Bílek, L. Drápal et al., *Notáský ád a ízení o dědictví (Notaries Rules and the Inheritance Proceedings*) (C.H. Beck, 2018); A. Macková, *Česká advokacie a vstup České republiky do EU* (*The Czech Bar and Access of the Czech Republic to EU*) in Czech Law in the EU (Iuridica: Acta Universitatis Carolinae 1-2/2004); A. Macková, *Právní pomoc* (*historické ko eny a ešení*), ('*The Legal Aid – Historical Roots and Solutions*'), in The Recodification of the Private Law (Iuridica: Acta Universitatis Carolinae, 1-2/2003); A. Macková, *Law on Attornyes*, C.H. Beck, 2017, Prague.

59. There are a number of statutory provisions and professional regulations concerning the organization of 'law firms' in the Czech Republic (www.cak.cz):

- Act on the Attorneys, Act No. 85/1996 Coll. as amended, provides the rules of enrolment to the Bar, regulates rights and duties of attorneys, the organizations of the Bar, the position of the lawyers from other EU Member State countries and the position of the lawyers, whose licence comes from other countries, the procedures under disciplinary offence and details on law firms' organization.
- A Code of Professional Conduct and Rules of Competition was issued and adopted by the Bar itself. Concerning law firms' organization, the Code provides rules of cooperation between attorneys (proper name of the law office and promotion rules for attorneys).
- The European dimension of attorneys' services has also influenced the Czech Bar. The EC Directives (No. 77/249, No. 89/48 and No. 98/5) were in successive steps reflected and implemented in the Czech law on attorneys' services. Attorneys from non-EU countries are entitled to provide legal services in the Czech Republic as 'foreign attorneys'. Their licence entitles them to provide limited legal services. The subject of legal service of a foreign attorney in the Czech Republic can only be the law of the country in which he/she is enrolled and international law.

II. Rights and Duties

60. The rights and duties of the attorneys are stipulated by the Code on Attorneys, by the CPC and other Procedural Laws and the professional regulation (e.g., Rules on Competition and the Ethical Code – *see* www.cak.cz). The primary duty of the attorney is to protect the rights and legal interests of the client. The attorney is obliged to maintain the secrecy (which covers all the information provided during the legal service for the clients (excepting money laundering fight and tax duties). The attorney is generally obliged to provide legal services (except conflict of interests and betrayal of trust between him/her and client), and he/she is entitled to get a fee. For those who can get the service of attorney, there is a system of legal aid (provided by the Bar or by the courts).

There is a full civil liability of the attorney to the client, he /she has to have a proper insurance contract, and the minimum insurance cover is stipulated. The attorneys have full criminal liability.

III. Discipline

61. The disciplinary power over the attorneys is entrusted to a profession itself. The disciplinary wrongdoing (offence) of the attorney means culpable breaching of his/her duties, when it is a serious one or repeated. The special disciplinary bench will hear the case after when submitted by the disciplinary plaintiff (the president of the council of control of the bar or the Minister of Justice). The penalization could be a warning, a public warning, fine, suspension or the strike off the list of attorneys.

62. All allowed organizational forms of law firms are used in the Czech Republic. Attorneys are allowed to perform advocacy as an independent practitioner, or to associate themselves in a partnership or a company (public company). An attorney can use only one of these allowed forms. Additionally, law firms can cooperate on an ad hoc or permanent basis.

The law on attorneys allows the independent practising of an attorney. This is the original form that the profession had. Later, in the development of the profession, it naturally developed that attorneys would begin to have greater cooperation. The independent performance of the profession has considerable advantages and disadvantages. The independence and liberty of an attorney are deeply wedded with the risks (i.e., an illness of the attorney, etc.). The law on attorneys postulates that the independent practising attorney has to have a substitute in case of any impediments to the performance of his/her duties and responsibilities (lasting more than one month). If the substitute is not chosen by an attorney, the Bar will appoint one on his/her behalf. If the independent practising attorney is stricken from the roll, the Bar will adopt measures to protect the rights and interests of that attorney's clients (i.e., appoint a successor of the attorney).

63. A partnership of attorneys is not a corporation. The partnership is generally regulated in the Civil Code, but there are some differences regulated by the law on attorneys, which reflect the nature of the profession.

64. Attorneys in the Czech Republic can associate themselves for the common performance of the profession and to create a company.

The general regulations on these companies are in the Code on Corporations. The law on attorneys regulates the relevant differences, which have to be observed by the attorneys, when they intend to establish such a company. The subject (activity) of such a company can only be to supply legal services. The companions (members) of such a company can only be attorneys. The company can supply legal services (advocacy), and it is subject to obligations arising from the provision of these same services. Even the delivery of the mail is legally relevant if it is delivered to the company. For the attorneys – companions of the company – there are no exclusions of the rights, duties and limitations generally postulated for attorneys. All the rights, duties and limitations are relevant for the company appropriately (i.e., to protect the rights and interests of clients, to maintain ethical rules, to maintain secrecy, the liability to the client, etc.).

The legal regime of the company of attorneys has to be adjusted to the nature and profession of the Bar as the Bar has a special nature different from that of companies (in general); therefore, the nature of a company of the attorneys must be adjusted to the profession of the Bar. Should one of the companions (an attorney) pass away the heir of that companion can only become a companion of the company if he/she is an attorney.

65. An attorney can cooperate on a permanent basis or as a substitute. Substitution is the right of an attorney to be replaced in the individual client's legal action by another attorney. The obligations, resulting from the substitution, can never limit the duties consequential from the oath or a professional regulation. Such cooperation can never limit (restrain) the independence of an attorney. It is an urgent duty to inform each other (between attorneys) in this cooperation to avoid a conflict of interest. The use of acquired information for the benefit of an attorney or third parties is not allowed.

An attorney can work for any other attorney, law firm or company (and foreign company) of attorneys as an employee (*see* Article 15a of Law on Attorneys), but just for one of those.

66. The name of a law office is strictly regulated by the law and professional regulations (Rules on Competition). The name of an attorney consists of compulsory components, permitted components (scientific titles) and subsidiary components (e.g., preferred fields of law; a cooperation with experts, translators, tax advisors or patent representatives or auditors; and other provided services connected with legal services like the arbiter or providing legal services in other languages). Compulsory components are name and family name and 'advokát, advokátka or advokátní kancelá' (or its equivalent under the regulations for European or foreign attorneys). If there is a partnership or company, compulsory components are the name and family name of at least one of the partners or companions and some of the following labelling like – 'advokáti', 'advokátní kancelá', 'sdružení advokát', ' ... a partnei', ' ... a společníci' or ' společnost advokát').

The academic or scientific titles and titles such as 'professor' or 'docent' or the indications about the succession are allowed. The names and the family names of the partners and companions who finish their activities can be preserved in the title if the requisite regulation is observed. If the attorney is entitled to provide legal services in another country, his/her name can also make use of the labelling which is used in that country.

The subsidiary indications for the law office can be the information that the attorney is an enrolled court expert or certified court translator, he/she is entitled to provide legal services in another country, any permanent cooperation with other attorneys and the place of business and affiliates.

In the case of business correspondence, it is necessary to use the name which the attorney chooses.

In addition to the Czech language of the labelling, the components can also be in the language of the country in which the attorney is entitled to provide legal services.

One of the ways to act and be perceived as an attorney is to be an employee of another attorney or a company of attorneys (one only). If the attorney chooses such a path, he/she will be known as an 'advokát' for the name of the attorney or company he/she is working for as an employee. An employed attorney is not allowed to employ another attorney or attorney trainee.

67. Czech attorneys are not enrolled under the localization principle. Any attorney can represent a party in litigation before any applicable court.

68. The legal profession is entitled to provide services in all the branches of law. But there is specialization within the profession in practice. The professional regulation presupposes the specialization (it can be reflected in the name and labelling of the law office – *see* above). The right of an attorney to refuse a client is relevant in connection with the preference that he/she has for certain fields of law and his/her professional experience.

69. The Czech legal system regulates the activities of tax consultants (Act No. 523/1992 Coll. on the Tax Consultants, as amended) and patent representatives (Act No. 417/2004 Coll. on the Patent Representatives). The regulations entitle tax consultants and patent representatives to provide services in their field of expertise to their clients. The notaries and the executors are also entitled to provide legal services to a limited extent (besides their main activities). There are traditional and deep-seated incompatibilities among these professions.

70. The European Economic Interest Grouping was introduced by an EC Regulation in 1985, and it represents the new legal entity for supranational cooperation of companies. The European Economic Interest Grouping was incorporated into the Czech legal system by Act No. 360/2004 Coll.

Chapter 3. Bailiffs

71. The enforcement of debts, which are substantiated by court judgments, can be realized in two different legal regimes: the enforcement can be conducted by either court enforcement or an executor (a special legal profession) can perform it. Court enforcement is described herein, and the position of executors is explained herein, as well.

At Czech courts, the following positions are established: higher court clerk, judge trainee, executor (as an employee of the court), assistant of the judge and secretary of the court office. The higher court clerk, trainee, assistant of the judge and executor are entitled under law to perform some actions of the court during litigation and execution.

Part II. Jurisdiction

Chapter 1. Domestic Jurisdiction

§1. Subject Matter Jurisdiction

I. Factors to Be Taken into Account

72. The Czech civil procedure law and doctrine strictly distinguishes between the notion of 'civil competence of courts' and the notion of 'jurisdiction of courts'. Both categories are viewed independently and individually, and both constitute one of the so-called procedural conditions (i.e., conditions subject to which only the court may decide on the merits of a case). The court reviews these conditions ex officio, i.e., without any motion by the parties. The defendant, however, may always use the procedural defence regarding procedural conditions; for example, he/she may challenge both the court's lack of competence and lack of jurisdiction.

The competence includes those matters that the courts are both entitled and obliged to hear and decide. Private law disputes (adversary matters) and other matters of private law (non-adversary matters) are the basis of the scope of the civil court competence. The Code of Civil Procedure defines civil competence in Article 7 as a competence to consider and decide matters arising from private law (e.g., civil, labour, intellectual property rights, family and business and commercial relationships).

The same Article 7 of the Code of Civil Procedure speaks about two derogations from the general definition: the competence may be narrowed or broadened by law.

73. Civil competence of the court is narrowed when certain matters are removed from the power of the court and placed in other, usually administrative proceedings. By way of example, let us mention decisions made by the Land Registry Office in keeping with Act No. 256/2013 Coll. on Land Register (cadaster). Such administrative decisions regarding ownership titles (and other titles to immovable property) are subject to judicial review in compliance with Part Five of the Code of Civil Procedure (in that special form of the administrative judiciary).

Civil competence of courts may be broadened whenever courts are given power to decide in matters other than private law matters. Such is the case in capital markets matters (in special non-adversary proceedings).

74. Civil court's competence may be excluded by the will of the parties if parties decide to take their dispute to an arbitrator instead of the court. The Act No.

216/1994 Coll. on Arbitration Proceedings and Enforcement of Arbitral Award regulates arbitration proceedings in the Czech Republic. Under this Act, parties may enter into a written agreement which may be either an agreement on the arbitrator (*compromise*) or an arbitration clause (*clause compromissoire*). Arbitration agreements may be entered into regarding property disputes in such matters which would allow for a judicial conciliation. The possibility of the judicial conciliation thus becomes the main criterion as to whether an arbitration agreement is or is not possible (arbitrability of the case). Consumer protection cases are not arbitrable in the Czech legal system since December 2016. In addition, the arbitration agreement is excluded in connection with disputes arising out of execution proceedings and bankruptcy proceedings, where the court's competence is exclusive. Valid arbitration agreement excludes civil court's competence.

75. Any individual with legal capacity or a permanent arbitration tribunal may be appointed as an arbitrator. The permanent arbitration tribunal may be established only by law. At present, there are three permanent arbitration tribunals in the Czech Republic: Arbitration Court attached to the Economic Chamber of the Czech Republic and the Agrarian Chamber of the Czech Republic, Arbitration Court attached to the Securities Exchange Prague Arbitration Court attached to the Czech Moravian Commodity Exchange Kladno.

76. Jurisdiction of the court is determined as a set of matters which may be decided on certain levels of the court system (jurisdiction in rem, venue jurisdiction) or by specific courts (territorial jurisdiction).

II. Main Claim and Ancillary Claims

77. Jurisdiction in rem determines which courts serve as the courts of first instance in which matters. These may be either district or regional courts unless the law provides otherwise.

The jurisdiction in rem is defined by law in detail (by the enumeration of cases which are in the jurisdiction of the Regional Court as a court of first instance, Article 9 section 2 of the Code of Civil Procedure).

78. The basic rule is contained in Article 9 section 1 of the Code of Civil Procedure: Unless provided otherwise by law, jurisdiction in rem in the first instance belongs to the district courts. Jurisdiction in rem of the district courts is the rule from which other provisions are an exception shifting the jurisdiction in rem upon regional courts.

79. There are numerous such exceptions by way of example; regional courts have jurisdiction in rem in connection with some difficult cases which require judges' specialization (such as, intellectual property matters, disputes in connection with retirement or health insurance). In commercial cases, regional courts' jurisdiction includes unfair competition, economic competition, all status-related matters of business companies and disputes between their authorized representatives, bankruptcy proceedings, etc.

80. Different jurisdiction in rem excludes consolidation of matters and mutual litigation since jurisdiction in rem must always be adhered to. Divergence from jurisdiction in rem gives grounds for an appeal. Conflicts regarding jurisdiction in rem between district and regional courts initiated by that court where the action was filed are dealt with by the High Court or by the Supreme Court (section 104a of the Code of Civil Procedure). Parties may address the issue of jurisdiction in rem; however, it is the court which decides.

81. Finally, it should be noted that specialized regional commercial courts were established after 1991 whose jurisdiction in rem only covered commercial cases (causal jurisdiction in rem). Excessive specialization proved ineffective, and the courts were abolished after several years.

III. Overview of the Different Courts

82. There are no special courts with the special jurisdiction in the Czech Judicial system besides the general courts (with civil and criminal jurisdictions); there is a Constitutional Court (*see* www.usoud.cz) controlling the conformity of the acts with the Constitution and the Supreme Administrative Court (*see* www. nssoud.cz) controlling the legality of the acts of the public administration authorities.

§2. Venue (Territorial Jurisdiction)

I. Factors to Be Taken into Account

83. There are specific rules to determine the venue of litigation, i.e., a specific court which has jurisdiction in a particular matter. The system of rules on venue consists of the general rules, which are supplementary if there is no special rule (which excludes the general rule).

A generally recognized rule says that a court of general jurisdiction located in the district of the party against which the action is directed (the defendant's domicile) is the venue (*actor sequitur forum rei*). The domicile is understood to be the place of permanent residence of an individual, and it is understood that one person may have several residences and, therefore, be subject to several venues. For entrepreneurs, the seat of their business determines the venue. Persons without residence fall under the territorial jurisdiction of general courts in the place of their usual whereabouts.

84. General courts having jurisdiction over legal persons are determined according to the seat of the legal persons. In the case of the State, the general court is determined based on the seat of the government body or entity concerned (such as a ministry).

85. In special cases, the venue may be derived from the last known domicile of a person, or determined by the fact that the defendant holds property in a district of a general court, or by the seat of a representative office or a branch office of a foreign company in the Czech Republic (Articles 84–86 of the Code of Civil Procedure).

Whenever the venue is impossible to determine, a motion may be made to the Supreme Court of the Czech Republic for such determination to be made.

In addition to a general venue, the Czech legal system also recognizes special territorial jurisdiction which may be either obligatory (exclusive) or alternative (optional).

86. Obligatory venue is given for non-adversary proceedings, such as matters of personal status, inheritance proceedings, custody of the court and court-administered registries, as well as for some adversary matters in which a particular reason exists for a different venue arrangement. For instance, disputes regarding immovable property have the venue in the district where the property is located – *locus rei sitae*, or disputes which are connected, such as disputes stemming out of execution or bankruptcy proceedings have a venue at the court that carries out the execution or the bankruptcy. All these exceptions are enumerated in Article 88 of the Code of Civil Procedure.

II. Main Claims and Ancillary Claims

87. Alternative venue gives the claimant a possibility to choose between the court of general jurisdiction and another court (such as the court of the place of payment in cases involving assertion of rights arising from a bill of exchange or a cheque, or the court of the seat of the stock exchange if it concerns disputes arising from a stock exchange deal), which might be more effective (money and time saving) for the claimant in a particular case. These options are set forth in Article 87 of the Code of Civil Procedure.

The venue rules apply equally to matters connected with the main action and to cross action by the defendant. This is without prejudice to special obligatory venue that must be always adhered to.

As a rule, venue is determined according to the circumstances at the time of the initiation of the proceedings, and the same venue continues until the end of the dispute (*perpetuatio fori*).

III. Overview of the Different Rules (And a Functional Jurisdiction)

88. In commercial matters, a written agreement of the parties regarding venue is permissible (prorogation). Such agreement must be filed together with the action and again without prejudice to obligatory venue.

§3. Functional Jurisdiction

89. Functional jurisdiction determines which courts hear the disputes in which instance. Functional jurisdiction is very simple when it concerns appeals. If a district court rules as a Court of First Instance, the functional jurisdiction over the appeal belongs to the superordinate Regional Court. If a Regional Court hears the case as a Court of First Instance (*see* jurisdiction in rem above), the functional jurisdiction over the appeal belongs to the respective higher court, i.e., High Court.

As regards extraordinary remedies, it is the Supreme Court of the Czech Republic that has functional jurisdiction over all extraordinary-appeal reviews. The other two extraordinary means of remedy have a form of action. In case of action for a retrial, that court which ruled in the first instance has functional jurisdiction. The same applies to the action for nullity. Here, however, some exceptions apply which sometimes give jurisdiction to the appellate court. (Article 235a(1) of the Code of Civil Procedure).

§4. Resolution of Jurisdiction and Competence Conflicts

90. Lack of competence or lack of jurisdiction may be reviewed upon the motion of a party (other than the claimant) or ex officio by the court due to that it is a proper procedure prerequisite.

In case of a lack of civil competence, the court which received the action shall end the proceedings and shall refer the case to the appropriate authority after its ruling ending the proceedings has become final (section 104 of the Code of Civil Procedure). The ruling ending the proceedings may be appealed.

Lack of jurisdiction in rem is at present reviewed directly by a higher court or the Supreme Court of the Czech Republic, and its findings are final in that regard (section 104a of the Code of Civil Procedure). This is a measure that has been adopted in order to expedite proceedings. Neither district nor regional courts may rule on the lack of jurisdiction in rem. In doubts, they refer the matter to the higher court (*see* above).

91. As regards venue, the basic rule provides that a lack of territorial jurisdiction is considered irrelevant unless it is recognized prior to the court's dealing with the merit of the case. A party may raise an objection for a lack of venue even later (and the court must rule on such objection), but there is a time limitation: an objecting party must do so no later than when performing its first act in the proceedings (section 105 of the Code of Civil Procedure). This provision secures that the issue of venue shall not be raised later in the proceedings, and the court shall be able to concentrate on the merits of the case. If the court establishes that it lacks territorial jurisdiction, it shall refer the case to the court which has such jurisdiction. An appeal against such decision is permissible.

92. In connection with the reform of administrative judiciary and with the establishment of the Supreme Administrative Court (*see* above), the Act No. 131/2002 Coll. was adopted regarding certain jurisdiction and competence conflicts. This Act applies to competence and jurisdiction conflicts between courts and executive bodies (competence) or between civil and administrative proceedings (jurisdiction in rem). Such conflicts are reviewed by a panel comprised of three judges from the Supreme Court and three judges from the Supreme Administrative Court.

Any party to a jurisdiction conflict (court, government or self-government body) may motion for the commencement of the proceedings, or a party to the dispute from which the jurisdiction conflict arose may do so. The finding of the special panel on the jurisdiction conflict is final.

Chapter 2. International Jurisdiction

§1. Rules Applicable in the Absence of a Treaty

93. As is the case in other countries, Czech courts have the general power to decide property disputes as well as non-contradictory matters involving a foreign or international element (a cross-border element). Matters involving an international element are considered to be cases in which one party is a foreign national or a foreign entity, or the object of the legal relation is located in a foreign country, or the legal relation was created in a foreign country and possibly also those matters a party to which is domiciled in a foreign country.

94. The courts always apply domestic procedure (lex fori) regardless of which substantive law is used; there are only several procedural derogations and special procedural rules. In particular, the issue of competence and jurisdiction is covered. All these rules regarding civil procedure with international element are centralized in one piece of legislation, the Act No. 91/2012 Coll. on International Private Law and International Civil Procedure (hereinafter 'IPLP').

It needs to be emphasized that provisions of the Act on IPLP are applied as subsidiary unless an international treaty with which the Czech Republic is bound provides otherwise. Bilateral and multilateral international treaties always prevail.

95. The principal conflict rule as far as procedure is concerned is Article 6 of IPLP which gives the Czech courts competence over property disputes provided the courts have jurisdiction in keeping with the Czech law (*see* above, issues of competence and jurisdiction). In property disputes with an international element, the competence of courts may also stem from prorogation, or competence may be given to arbitrators by way of an agreement.

96. Special provisions have been made regarding the competence of Czech courts (given the presence of an international element) in particular private law matters in Articles 29–101 of IPLP.

The Act No. 91/2012 Coll. on IPLP also contains cases of exclusions from the competence of Czech courts (immunity). Thus foreign governments are exempt as well as individuals who enjoy immunity in the Czech Republic based on international agreements or other applicable rules, such as diplomatic rules (*see* Article 7 of IPLP).

97. In the proceedings with an international (cross-border) element, Czech courts proceed in compliance with the Czech civil procedure. Procedural capacity of a foreign national (i.e., the capacity to stand before the court) is governed by the procedural rules of his home State. It, however, suffices if he/she has procedural capacity according to the Czech law. Foreign nationals might be exempt from court fees and advance payments on request and have the right to free legal counsel subject to reciprocity. If a foreign national is in the position of a petitioner in a property dispute, he/she may be ordered to put down a security deposit upon the defendant's motion (with some dispensations). For evidence taking, it is stipulated that public documents issued by courts and authorities in a foreign country have the same force as public documents issued domestically.

The issue of recognition and enforcement of foreign judgments in the Czech Republic is discussed in Part IX, Chapter 2.

§2. International Treaties

98. In its Article 10, the Constitution of the Czech Republic provides that ratified international treaties, approved by the Parliament and binding on the Czech Republic, become an integral part of the Czech legal order. In case of conflict between the international treaty and the domestic law, the international treaty prevails.

The Czech Republic is a party to many bilateral and multilateral international treaties which are subject to the above constitutional provision. Bilateral agreements on mutual legal assistance have been entered into with most European and some overseas countries.

99. The multilateral treaties with relation to civil procedure include: the Convention on Civil Procedure concluded in the Hague on 1 March 1954, the Convention on the Service Abroad of Judicial and Extrajudicial Documents in Civil and Commercial Matters concluded in the Hague on 15 November 1956 and the Convention on Taking of Evidence Abroad in Civil or Commercial Matters concluded in the Hague on 18 March 1970. Today, these treaties have relevance only vis-à-vis parties from outside the European Union.

100. At the present time of intensive integration within the European Union, the issues at hand are different. Originally stemming from international conventions, the law of the EU today converts into secondary legislation which replaces the said international treaties. As a member of the EU as of 1 May 2004, the Czech Republic is bound by European legislation directly. That is true for the Regulations listed below.

101. In civil procedure, the Czech Republic is bound by:

(1) EU Regulation No. 1215/2012 (Brussels I bis, the current version of the Brussels Convention I, on jurisdiction, recognition and enforcement of judgments in civil and commercial matters).
(2) EU Regulation No. 2201/2003 (the current version of the Brussels Convention II, on the jurisdiction, recognition and enforcement of judgments in matrimonial matters).
(3) EU Regulation No. 1393/2007 (the original Convention on the delivery of documents in civil and commercial matters).
(4) EU Regulation No. 848/2015 (Convention on insolvency proceedings).
(5) EU Regulation No. 1206/2001 (on cooperation between the courts of the Member States in the taking of evidence in civil or commercial matters).

(6) EU Regulation No. 805/2004 (on European Enforcement Order for uncontested claims).
(7) EU Regulation No. 1896/2006 (on European order for payment procedure).
(8) EU Regulation No. 861/2007 (on European Small Claim Procedure).
(9) EU Regulation No. 650/2012 (on Heritage).

102. In addition to that, the Czech Republic is currently in the process of transposing into its domestic legislation provisions on further obligations stemming from the EU membership. These include for instance provisions of Article 109 section d) of the Code of Civil Procedure on the suspension of the proceedings based on the court's decision to pose a preliminary question to the European Court of Justice (ECJ) in compliance with Article 35 of the EU Treaty.[4]

4. A. Winterová, A. Macková et al., *Civilní právo procesní* (*The Civil Procedure Law*) 9th edn. (Leges Praha a.s., 2018), p. 215.

Part III. Actions and Claims

Chapter 1. Actions

§1. Definition

103. The relation between the substantive and procedural law is the relation between the two independent branches of law; there is no writs system. The fundamental way of opening of the litigation is the action (exceptionally, the litigation can be initiated without the action of the party – *see* Article 81 of CPC). The action is a pronouncement of the right to litigation (*ius ad litem*) and the general meaning of the protection of the rights. The action is the procedural act of the party, by which he/she asks the court to protect his/her rights and to lawfully pass the final sentence. The compulsory essentials of the action are the parties, subject of the claim and its reasoning. The action has its general essentials (to which court it is addressed, who is the plaintiff, what is the demand) and its special essential (details on parties, the relevant statements on factual respect of the case, the evidence and the proposal for the sentence). The special essentials are the pronouncement of the contradictory principle because by the realization of this essential is the fulfilment of the two basic procedural duties, the duty to declare facts and the duty to propose the evidence to prove the facts he/she declares.

The due time submitted action with all the essentials causes the legal (procedural and substantive law) effects. The procedural effects are the arising of the special duty to the court to perform litigation (otherwise it would be *denegatio iustitiae* – the illegal refusal of the protection of the rights). In the substantive law, the action means the suspension of the preclusion of rights. The date of the opening of the litigation is the day in which the action was delivered to the court. The action is a pronouncement of the principle of the disposition: the claimant has the power of disposition of the litigation. Beside the disposition of the litigation, there is power to perform other acts of disposition: drawing down of the action (in extenso or in part), as long as the Court of Appeal passes a judgment. The court suspends the litigation in such a case, as a case may be the court will abolish the passed (but not lawful) judgment. After the judgment is lawful, the drawn down of the claim is not effective. The drawn down of the action will not be effective if the other parties do not agree.

The claimant has the power to dispose of the subject of the litigation: he/she can change his/her action. The change of the action can be made only with the permission of the court. The court will not permit the change of the action if the results of present litigation would not serve for the litigation on the changed subject (the economy of the procedure).

§2. Admissibility (Standing)

104. Before a decision of the court on the merit of a case is issued, the court examines the admissibility (the procedural prerequisite which the court must observe ex officio). The prerequisites are partly positive (that must be fulfilled) and partly negative (that must be absent). The procedural prerequisites are related either to the court, to the parties, or to the subject matter in dispute.

The court must be competent (within the meaning of international jurisdiction, local competence/venue/and subject matter/jurisdiction in rem/competence).

The parties must have a capacity to be parties and conduct legal acts. The capacity to be a party pertains to everyone who has legal personality under the substantive law. The capacity to conduct legal acts either personally or through a chosen representative is coextensive with the capacity to enter into contracts (which is determined by the substantive law). If there is a lack of capacity to conduct legal acts, the party must have statutory representative (a parent or a trustee), who must have both above-mentioned capacities, and the power of representative must be proved.

There is, however, no duty for parties to be represented in the court by an attorney, with exception to litigation on extraordinary appeals before the Supreme Court.

There are negative prerequisites relating to the subject matter; that is, the claim must not be object of another litigation pending (*litis pendentia* – *see* Article 83 paragraph 1 of CPC) or not even be res iudicata (*see* Article 159a paragraph 5 of CPC) The same parties may not litigate the same claim twice (whether in the same or in the other court).

105. The negative prerequisite for the litigation in court is also existing *arbitration agreement* (*see* Article 106 of CPC). The defendant may object the existence of this agreement at his/her first procedural act (motion) in the litigation. The court subsequently will suspend the litigation in such a case.

The prerequisites are examined by the court permanently during the proceedings (with exception of the local competence – venue) and if there is a lack of some prerequisite, the court will consider if the litigation can continue or if it must be suspended without decision on subject matter (*see* Article 107 of CPC), because the lack is indelible.

Chapter 2. Claims and Defences

§1. Claims: Definition And Distinctions

106. The plaintiff can claim any kinds of requirements. The claim is the content of the action (*see* Article 79 of CPC). It is the imperative of the principle of disposition (and the principle of the autonomy of the will) to express the claim accurately. It is the autonomous will of the plaintiff to claim whatever he/she wants and to whichever extent. He or she, however, must support the claim by exact statements of relevant facts so the court can find proper legal qualification (to find and to apply appropriate regulation).

The plaintiff is not obliged to perform the legal qualification of his/her claim. His/her procedural duties consist in declaring of statements (factual) and providing of evidence to that statements.

The actions can be differentiated under the claims it involved:

(1) an action for the performance of any behaviour (to give, to do, to restrain, to endure any behaviour);
(2) an action for the determination (i.e., who is the owner of the immovable, etc.);
(3) an action under which the court issues the judgment, which constitutes a new legal relationship (i.e., judgment on settlement of the divided co-ownership).

The claims of the actions can be differentiated under its formulation. The claim of the action can be:

(1) simple (contains only one claim); and
(2) composed (contains two or more claims).

107. The composed claim of the action can be formulated as:

(1) Alternative claim, the plaintiff indicates his/her will to accept any of the suggested behaviour of the defendant. The court will (if the plaintiff will win the case) issue a judgment with both of the suggested behaviours. The defendant can choose one of them.
(2) Eventual claim, the plaintiff indicates the second behaviour of the defendant for the situation – as the case may be during the litigation, the first behaviour of the defendant is not objectively possible (the thing does not exist, the work is not possible to perform and the like). The court will issue a judgment which commands the defendant to perform only either the first suggested behaviour or the subsidiary behaviour.

Alternativa facultas is the plaintiff's proposal (via action) to the defendant; he can disengage his duties by the other behaviour. The court will issue the judgment in accordance with the formulation of the claim.

The claims can be cumulated in the action, even if it is supported by different reasons (the plaintiff can ask the defendant for to return an object and to pay compensation for damage, or the defendants can be different persons – requisition of unpaid rent against different renters in the same dwelling).

The Czech law makes it possible to save time and costs (procedural economy) through a 'connection of the litigations' (*see* Article 112 of CPC).

The connection of litigation is possible if there is the same jurisdiction of the courts, both litigations are either adversary or non-adversary, and the composition of the court's bench is the same (an individual judge or a board of judges). There is compulsory connection of the litigations also (*see* Article 113 of CPC).

§2. Defences

108. The defendant can face the plaintiff's claims by the procedural defence or by the objections. These defences may be qualified by its merits: substantive objections or procedural objections. The claims, which the defendant has against the plaintiff, can be laid out in mutual action (counterclaim). A mutual action is a legal act of the defendant, which out steps the only procedural defence. The mutual action is stated in the same litigation, and it is possible to apply it whenever during first instance litigation. A mutual action must fulfil all the essentials specified for the action generally. If there is a mutual action, the court will connect both litigations, but it can be excluded from the separate litigation. In the connected litigation, the mutual action has its separate regime because it is not an objection to compensation.

§3. Vexatious Litigation

109. The Czech Civil Procedural law has no list of vexatious litigation. Any claim, thus, will be considered and evaluated in a proper way. The frivolous claims may result in a sanction to compensate costs of the defendant.

Chapter 3. Sanction on Procedural Irregularities

110. The litigating parties can violate their procedural duties. A violation of duties, which are the basis of the principle of contradictory (the duty to declare the facts and the duty to propose the evidence), has its reflection in the final judgment on subject merit because the party does not sustain the burden of statements or the burden of proof.

The violation of any other duties (i.e., non-payment of the court fee or lack of the essentials of the action) will conclude without a judgment on merit (the court will suspend the litigation because there is lack of determined prerequisites).

The procedural sanction might be however stronger: a special judgment by default. This judgment can be issued if the defendant misses the first hearing of the court in the case that he/she was properly informed and the plaintiff (who is present) proposes it. The factual statements, which the plaintiff performed in the action, are unquestionable for the court in such a case.

The default judgment can be abolished if it is proved that the defendant missed the hearing because of reasonable causes. If the cause for missing the hearing is considered reasonable, the court will abolish the issued judgment and will direct the hearing.

If the party makes the proceedings difficult (i.e., by being absent from court), by contempt of court or by other procedural offences, they can be punished with a maximum fine of CZK 50,000 (ca EUR 2,000). If there is a disturbance in the court, the violator can be banished from the courtroom, and the hearing will continue without his/her presence.

Special procedures are applied if there is a delay caused by the parties. The relevant changes were adopted in 2001 and 2009 into the CPC when the power of the court to address the delay of a party in litigation was fortified. The judge has the power to command the defendant (who causes the delay) to give his/her opinion on the action in a determined time limit with a sanction that the court will not consider the opinion/facts which will be delivered beyond that point (the concentration principle).[5]

5. A. Winterová, A. Macková et al., *Civilní právo procesní* (*The Civil Procedure Law*) 9th edn. (Leges Praha a.s., 2018), pp. 221 and f.; A. Winterová, *žaloba v právu procesním* (*The Action in Procedural Law*) (UK, Praha 1979).

Part IV. Proceedings

Chapter 1. Pretrial Proceedings

111. There is no regulation on pretrial proceedings in Czech Civil Procedural Law. The pretrial proceedings are more typical for common law system of law.

Before the litigation is open, however, the court may ratify the settlement of the dispute (a consent decree) to order a preliminary measure or to secure (future) evidence.

The ratification of a settlement is possible if the nature of the matter is permissible. It is fundamentally permissible in relations, which can be disposed of by the parties (typically the property relations).

The preliminary measures are issued and ordered prior to litigation is open or even after it is opened if there is a necessity to settle the relations or if there is a doubt the future execution will be successful. The court will decide on preliminary measures without hearing and in short time limits. The competent court is the same court, which would decide on the subject matter. The law strictly determines the essentials for such a proposal. If there is lack of these essentials, the court will disclaim the proposal. The preliminary measure can, i.e., command the duty to pay some sustenance, to give over the minor to another person or institution, to save some amount for deposit, etc.

The preliminary measure defines limitations and potential damages, the claimant is obliged to save CZK 10,000 (ca. EUR 400) or CZK 50,000 (ca. EUR 2,000) in commercial cases or amount, which is under court consideration appropriate with circumstances of the case) – as a bail security. There is a duty for the court to decide on a preliminary measure without any delay, at least seven days after the proposal was delivered to the court.

There is a special legal regime for preliminary measures that are concerned with children. The aim of the regulation is to find a solution for a child or endangered person as soon as possible without any delay. The court is obliged to decide at least within twenty-four hours.

Another special legal regime is for domestic violence protection. In such a case, the court is obliged to decide on violated person's claim within forty-eight hours.

The securing of the evidence is necessary if there is a doubt the evidence will not be disposable later in the litigation (i.e., the witness is leaving the country, the expert will be in hospital, etc.). The evidence will be secured when the court performs it in a proper way (i.e., hear a witness).

Chapter 2. Proceeding in First Instance

112. The litigation in first instance generally has the following stages: the submission of the action, the preparation of the hearing by the judge (including putting forth the opinion of the defendant and the preparation of the evidence), hearing and judgment.

§1. Adversary Proceedings

I. Ordinary Proceedings

A. *Introduction of the Claim*

113. The action must be delivered to the court with a sufficient number of copies (one copy will stay at the court, and every party will get one copy); the electronic form is allowed as well. The plaintiff is obliged to connect the action to the documentary evidence, which he/she proposes to examine.

Under the nature of the claim, the court will consider its jurisdiction and competence (local and on subject matter). Besides the other prerequisites, the court examines if the fee was paid. The plaintiff may ask for a release from this duty, or the law can release him/her.

The court in this stage of litigation also examines if the action has its essentials. If there is a lack of essentials, the plaintiff is called upon to complete the action. If the action is perfect, the litigation continues by the preparation of hearing.

The hearing is the part of the litigation with special relevancy. The court is in direct contact with the parties and evidence (the oral principle). The first instance litigation is fundamentally oral (with hearing). The hearing opens the possibility for the parties to answer immediately to the statements of the adversary, to the witnesses, to the experts, etc. The hearing of the court is public (the principle of the openness and public hearing). The public can be excluded only rarely, and the law defines such cases strictly (the protection of secrecy, the protection of relevant interests of the parties or the protection of morality). The court can also bar a certain person if he/she disturbs the dignity of the court hearing.

B. *Progress of Proceedings*

1. Preparatory Measures

114. The CPC declares the principle that the judge should prepare the hearing properly to finish the case after only one hearing (*see* Article 114a section 1). The preparation of the hearing is very important, and the CPC emphasizes this.

The court's preparation of the hearing comprises:

- the call upon the defendant to perform his/her written viewpoint and to submit all the proposed evidence;
- the requirement of the report on the facts relevant for litigation (*see* Article 128 of CPC);
- the assignation of the expert, if necessary; and
- the security of the feasibility to examine the evidence (or ask the cooperated court to examine evidence).

115. There is a possibility for the judge to fight off the delay caused by the defendant and instead of his/her viewpoint (or if he/she disobey it) the judge can command the defendant to provide his/her position and the facts and evidence in the determined time limit (minimum of thirty days after delivering of this decision of the court). This decision has special consequences, if there is no expression of the defendant within the time limit. The court, in such a case, will issue the final judgment on the merit (supported only by the statements of the plaintiff in the action – *see* Article 153a of CPC). Judge may also call a special preparatory hearing, purpose of which is to clear the subject of the evidence and to command the parties to propose evidence to the end of this hearing or within certain time limit.

The CPC regulates the procedure if any of hereinabove mentioned alternatives have no effect for the proper preparation of the hearing. In such situation, the court will call the parties (their representatives) to instruct them, try them to settle the dispute and ask them to amend the statements for continuing of the litigation.

2. Determination of the Trial Date and Oral Hearing

116. The hearing is to be summoned in due time because the parties must have ample time to prepare themselves properly. The time for the preparation is determined by the CPC, and it is minimum ten days generally.

Litigation without hearing is an exception. There is no hearing if it is possible to decide the case based on the submitted written evidence and if there is an agreement of both parties.

The hearing is open and administered by the judge. The judge recognizes the speeches, examines the evidence and carries out other measures. The judge has to keep the dignity and not disturb the hearing. The main aim of the hearing is to dispute the case completely, rightly and without delay.

The first speaker of the hearing is the plaintiff with his/her claims, and subsequently, the defendant will announce his/her written viewpoint. If the parties are not present, the judge will announce their positions. If necessary, the parties are asked to complete their expression.

After that, the judge will notify the results of the preparation of the hearing and designates the subject of the proofs and the evidence, which will be examined.

If the proposals of the facts and evidence are not complete, the court will ask them to supply it under proper instruction. The court will not consider the facts and evidence submitted after the expiration of the time limit.

It should be remembered that the parties in principle are not allowed to submit new facts and evidence for an appeal litigation; there is a limited appellation system for the adversary litigation (*see* Article 205a of CPC).

Fundamentally, the CPC pursues only one hearing in every litigation (*see* Article 114a section 1). Exceptionally there can be a suspension of the hearing. The court has to announce the considerable reasons for the suspension of the hearing. The parties should be informed about the date of the next hearing at the same time. The time limit for the preparation for the parties is in such cases is appropriately shorter.

117. Before the hearing is closed, the court will instruct the parties that there is only exceptional possibility to submit the facts and evidence for the appeal litigation and call them to submit it before the judgment is declared.

If there is no relevant fact or evidence, the court will ask the parties to summarize their viewpoints and proposals and to comment on the factual and legal point of the case.

The judge or the board of judges (after the consultation) will declare the judgment.

3. Not Advocate General or Amicus Curiae

118. The Czech civil procedure in principle does not work with the institution of the *advocate generale nebo* amicus curiae like in the French legal system or like at the Court of Justice of the EU.

C. Judgment

119. The judgment is the legal act of the court. It is the manifestation of the will of the procedural subject. The predicate of the judgment has the relevant and enforceable consequences – it is an authoritative predicate on subject merit or procedural points.

120. The judgment is created in some stages:

(1) The Resolving – the court establishes the content of the judgment (the board of the judges has its special rules for voting to avoid influencing and to ensure the secrecy of this procedure).
(2) The Declaration – after the judgment is resolved, it has to be announced to the parties. The subject of the publication is the predicate of the judgment, brief reasoning and instruction on how to appeal. The judgment has to declare on behalf of the State – *'Jménem republiky'* – which emphasizes the authority of the judgment and power of the judiciary. The declaration of the judgment is the publication of it. The declaration means mandatory consequences for the parties and the same time the court is bound by the published judgment. The declaration of the judgment must be made publicly in hearing (even if the

hearing was closed to public). The judgment in the matter of business competition, protection of the intellectual property or protection of the consumer might be (under the motion of the winner of the case) published widely and the cost of this publication is charged to the loosing party.

The parties are then asked if they recede from the right to appeal, which can project the written form of the judgment:

(1) The Drawing Up; following by
(2) The Delivering to the parties.

1. Different Kinds of Judgments

121. The predicate as a part of the decision observes the settlement of the legal situation – either merit or procedural. This implicates the two basic kinds of decisions: decisions on merit and procedural decisions.

Another division is constitutive judgment and declaratory judgment (under the effects of the judgments to the relations). The declaratory judgments declare with authority the status, which was established another way (to pay a debt, which arise from the contract). The constitutive judgments establish, abolish or change the relations. The declaratory judgment is the fundamental form of the judgment in civil adversary litigation because it reflects the principles and nature of the private law. The constitutive judgment is on the contrary exceptional and the possibility the court can issue it has to be established in the law.

Respecting the content of the predicate, the decisions can be classified into decisions which command to perform some legal behaviour, the decisions which determine if there is the relationship or right and the decisions on determinations of the legal status.

The decisions can be final, partial and interlocutory. The final decision covers all the subject of litigation and partially covers only the part of it and interlocutory decisions, which predicate covers only the legal base of the subject of the litigation. The interlocutory decision is purposeful to save the cost of the determination of the claim amount. Before the interlocutory decision is in the legal force, there is no spending of the costs (i.e., the interlocutory decision determines the defendant is liable to pay compensation of a damage, or the interlocutory decision determines the defendant is liable for the unlawful interference to the personality of somebody).

The court has to respect the relationship between the action and the predicate of the judgment which is assigned by the principle '*iudex ne eat ultra petita partium*', and the court cannot adjudicate more than the action is asking.

There are three formal kinds of decisions: the judgment, the ruling and the payment order.

The judgment is reserved for the decision on the matter. The ruling is in principle issued on procedural questions. It is allowed to issue a ruling on the matter, only if there is the special regulation (typically in non-adversary litigation).

The payment order is issued only in the special summary proceeding.

2. Formal Aspects of the Judgment

122. The writing (the drawing up) of the judgment is the next stage of its creation (after the resolving and the declaration). The written judgment is the document with special legal power.

The written form of judgment can be different. The basic structure is, however, the same. The judgment consists of the head, the predicate, the reasoning, the instruction and the date and the signature. There is a difference between the written form of the judgment and the written form of ruling. The written form of the judgment is more formal than the written form of ruling, which is issued on procedural issues. There are the names of the court and judges in the head of the judgment, the indication of the parties and the exact indication of the subject matter (which is relevant for examination of the res iudicata). There will be indicated also the kind of the certain judgment (partial judgment, judgment by default, etc.).

The predicate is the crucial part of the judgment. The court authoritatively determines the rights and duties of the parties in the predicate. If there is a duty to perform any behaviour in the predicate, the court has to assign the time limit, which fundamentally lasts three days after the legal force of the judgment. (The time limit could be assigned longer, or it can be allowed to pay off instalments).

The predicate of the judgment in principle contains the predicate on costs of litigation. Exceptionally, the court can decide on costs in the special ruling.

The reasoning of the judgment is as a rule its longest part. There is a legal requirement that the court should express the essence of the speeches and proposals of the parties, summarize proved and unproved facts, present which evidence supports the discovery (including the evaluation of the evidence in detail), sustain why no other proposed evidence was examined, and the parties must be provided the full explanation on the legal qualification of the matter of the case.

The default judgment and judgment for recognition of the debt have another kind of reasoning with the only subject of the litigation, and a reason for the special judgment was issued. The same applies to the judgment in case there is no appeal or if the parties recede from appeal.

The fundamental principle is the reasoning of the judgment has to be convincing and educational.

The instruction as a part of the judgment has to contain the instruction how to appeal (or that there is no appeal) and extraordinary appeal. There must be the instruction on the execution also (e.g., in non-adversary proceedings the divorced spouses are instructed to choose their previous name).

The written form of the ruling is simpler (this applies in particular for the rulings, which are not subject to the delivery to the parties).

The ruling in principle has a similar structure like the judgment but less comprehensive. Some rulings (which fully satisfy the proposal or rulings on procedure) may not be reasoned.

3. Delivering of the Judgment

123. The judgment (copy of it) is subject of the delivery. The judgment is fundamentally delivered personally. Some kinds of rulings are not the subject of the delivery (*see* Article 168 section 2 of CPC). If a party to the litigation has its data mailbox, there is a duty of the court to use this data box for electronic delivery (*see* Law No. 300/2008 Coll. on Electronic Communication).

The Judgment should be delivered at the court (after hearing the case) primarily. Subsequently, it will be delivered into a data box (if the party has such a data box), and the ultimate way of delivery is the delivery made by court-mailman (clerk of the court or Judicial Guard) or by the other party or its representative.

There is personal delivery or simply delivery under the Czech Civil Procedural Law.

The personal delivery covers the most important documents (a judgment primarily). There is protection against the gratuitous evade of documents by the legal fiction of delivery when evades. If the party have a reasonable reason, the court may pronounce the ineffectiveness of the delivery in such a cease.

The payment order has to be delivered personally invariably.

4. Res Iudicata

124. The written form of the judgment, delivered to the parties, has relevant legal effects.

The court is bound by its decision after its publication (see Article 156 section 3 of CPC). One of the effects of the legal force is the inconvertibility of the decision (material legal force and formal legal force – *see* Article 159a odst. 4 of CPC).

The legal forced decision establishes res iudicata impediment, and it is not allowed to contest it by the appeal. If there is no appeal allowed, res iudicata impediment comes on after the delivering of the judgment. If there is right to appeal, the res iudicata impediment comes on after the expiration of the time limit for the appeal or if the parties receded from the appeal.

The legal forced judgment can be contested only by the extraordinary remedies (retrial and nullity plea – *see* Article 228 and following of CPC, and extraordinary appeal – *see* Article 236 of CPC), which admissibility is strictly regulated.

The impediment res iudicata is being under consideration only with the judgments on merit. The other decisions are not such an impediment.

The extent of the res iudicata impediment is determined by the extent of the allegiance of the judgment (*see* Article 159a of CPC). Fundamentally, the judgment is binding the parties of the litigation.

125. The impediment res iudicata consists in the subject of the litigation can be the subject of the litigation again (except the extraordinary remedies). The identity of the subject of the litigation rests in the same parties of the litigation and the unvaried subject of the litigation. The court considers the impediment res iudicata ex officio. If the detection shows there is res iudicata, the litigation will be suspended (*see* Article 104 section 1 of CPC). The impediment res iudicata strengthens the legal certainty because it inhibits the existence of two or more decisions on the same matter.

5. Interpretation and Rectification of Judgments

126. The aim of the litigation is to settle the dispute authoritatively. This aim is addressed by the issued judgment on merit, and it has its reflection in the nature of the judgment in its legal force and enforceability.

The legal force comes on if the legal prerequisites are met. There is a formal legal force (in relations to litigation) and material legal force (in relation to the subject of the litigation). The formal legal force consists in the definitiveness of the judgment. The material legal force consists in cogency and inconvertibility of the judgment.

The formal legal force is determined in Article 159 of CPC. The judgment is under this Article in legal force if it is delivered and it can be contested by appeal.

The material legal force (*see* Article 159 of CPC) means the cogency of the judgment for the concerned persons.

The subjective limits of the judgment (*see* Article 159a of CPC) mean the judgment is cogent for the parties of the litigation and their successors. Also, the judgment obliges all the authorities (with the power to issue the authoritative decisions).

There are some judgments with the effects, erga omnes which exceed the parties of the litigation (the judgments on personal status – on divorce, on legal capacity or unfair competition, consumer protection, etc.).

The *actio popularis* is not generally permissible in the Czech civil procedure (*see* Article 83 sections 2 and 159a section 2 of CPC). The judgments on *actio popularis* have effects on not only the parties of the litigation but also the subjects entitled to sue the defendant on the same factual base.

The inconvertibility of a judgment (*see* Article 159a section 4 of CPC) means that the same matter cannot be the subject of the litigation again. The identity of the matter means the same parties and the same subject of litigation. The inconvertibility of the judgment is under consideration only for the judgments on merit. The procedural decisions (i.e., suspension of the litigation) are not the impediment of the new litigation.

The inconvertibility is not absolute. The judgment can be changed exceptionally through the extraordinary appeal and other extraordinary remedies.

The exception of the inconvertibility of the judgment is the judgment issued with the clause *rebus sic stantibus* (*see* Article 163 of CPC). The CPC establishes some cases in which the issued judgment can be changed not by the extraordinary remedies but in another way (e.g., in adoption cases, the judgment can be altered by way of a special procedure (Article 185 of CPC)).

The enforcement of the judgment is another feature of the judgment. The enforcement consists of the direct enforcement of the duty by the State power.

The enforcement of the judgment comes on after the expiration of the time limit for the performance of the duty. This time limit lasts in principle three days after the judgment's legal force (fifteen days after the legal force in cases of the vacation of the flat). The court may decide on a longer time limit or instalment payment.

There are the special judgments – preliminary enforceable judgments. As a rule applies to them, the time limit runs from the delivery of the judgment. The preliminary enforceable judgment means the possibility; it is enforceable before its legal force. This legal construction gives priority to the promptitude of the enforcement before the certainty, which is established by the judgment in legal force. The preliminary enforceable judgment is an advantage for the plaintiff because it guarantees faster access to the benefit. There are cases of compulsory preliminary enforceability of the judgments (the judgments on alimentation or the judgments on salary for the last three months before the judgment – *see* Article 162 section 2 of CPC). The preliminary judgments can be facultative issued when there is a risk of the considerable loss.

127. The judgment can be complemented or corrected not only by the post-trial remedies. If there are mistakes in typing or figures, the judgment will be corrected, even if there is a legal force. If the mistake is in the predicate of the judgment, the court will issue the special correcting ruling.

The reasoning can be deficient too (i.e., if the conclusion does not correspond to the litigation). The court will correct the reasoning under the party's proposal.

There can be a fault; the predicate does not contain all the statement. The court will issue (under the party's proposal or ex officio) the decision, which will complete the faulty predicate.

6. The Penalty in Case of Non-compliance with Judgments

128. If the judgment is not respected by the liable person, there is a right of the entitled person to propose the enforcement of the judgment by the court or to ask the executor to enforce the judgment. The execution cannot be initiated without the proposal of the entitled person, which corresponds to the principle of party autonomy.

II. Provisional Proceedings

129. The default judgment and judgment on recognition of the debt are issued after the special litigation. This litigation has a simplified procedure, which reflects that both judgments are issued without the discovery of the factual respect of the matter. The law strictly regulates the prerequisites for its issuing. Its reasoning is simplified too (it consists of the subject of matter and brief reasoning as to why it was issued).

§2. Default Proceedings

130. The default judgment can be issued if the defendant misses the first hearing of the court, even when he/she was properly convened and if the plaintiff is present at hearing and he/she proposes such a judgment should be issued. The court as an unquestionable in such a case considers the factual statements, which the plaintiff performed in the action.

The default judgment can be abolished if it is proved (before its legal force) that the defendant's missing of the hearing was justified by reasonable causes. If the cause of the missing is considered as reasonable, the court will abolish the issued judgment and will direct the hearing.

§3. Ex Parte Proceedings

131. The civil litigation is dominated by the principles of orality, directness and public hearing (*see* Article 116 of CPC).

Therefore fundamentally there is a hearing within the litigation (*see* Article 115 section 1 of CPC). Exceptionally, the hearing cannot be called, if all the legal prerequisites are observed like the adversary nature of the matter, etc. (*see* Article 115a).

The other case of the litigation without hearing is the will of the parties, and the court can support its judgment on the written evidence, which was submitted by the parties.

132. The preliminary measures are issued without hearing as well. There is, however, a duty for the plaintiff to make a deposit as a caution. Preliminary measures are issued before the litigation is open or even after it is open, if there is a necessity to settle the relations or if there is a doubt the future execution will be successful. The court will decide on preliminary measures without a hearing and in short time limits. The law strictly determines the requirements for such a proposal. If the requirements are not met, the court will disclaim the proposal. A preliminary measure can result in an order to pay some support or to hand over a minor to another person or institution or to set aside some amount for deposit, etc.

The preliminary measure determines limitations and potential damages. The plaintiff, therefore, has a special duty to deposit CZK 10,000 – or CZK 50,000 in commercial cases (or other amounts appropriate to the circumstances of the case under court consideration) – as a bail security deposit. The court has a duty to decide on the preliminary measure without any delay: at least seven days after the proposal was delivered to the court. The bail security will be returned to the plaintiff, for example, if the proposal was refused (*see* Article 77a sections 1 and 2 of CPC). In certain exceptional cases, the court does not ask for bail security. These cases are regulated by Article 75b section 3 of CPC. The court will not require bail security if the plaintiff is socially deprived (he/she could be subject to an exemption of security under Article 138 of CPC). The court cannot ask for bail security if there are urgent time restraints or if the plaintiff can prove that the deposit of bail will damage them greatly.

Chapter 3. Review Proceedings

§1. Appeal

133. The appeal is a judicial remedy, by which the decision of the court of the first instance (the judgment and ruling) can be contested before it is final (legal force).

An appeal is fundamentally widely admissible, and the inadmissibility of an appeal is exceptional. The conditions of admissibility are objective and subjective. An appeal is excluded against certain judgments and rulings. A judgment on small debts (*bagatelle*) is not possible to contest by an appeal. As a pecuniary entitlement, the law characterizes small debts as being under CZK 10,000–ca. EUR 380 (the accessories of the debt are not considered). A default judgment and a judgment on recognition of debt also have a special regime for appeal. An appeal is not admissible against a number of rulings. For the most part, as far as procedural ruling are concerned, they cannot cause any serious prejudice to the parties.

Only the predicate can be the subject of an appeal. The time limit for the appeal is fifteen days after the decision was delivered to the party. The entitled subject of the appeal is the party who lost the case or the subsidiary participant and the public prosecutor (as the case may be).

There are requirements stated by the law for an appeal. The general requirements are to which court it is addressed, who the appellant is and what is the aim of the appeal. The special essential is the specification of the contested judgment, the extent of the appeal, some of the stated reasons for the appeal and the proposal. The appeal in the Czech civil procedure reflects the principle of the limited appellation. This principle limits the appellant to submit 'new' facts and evidence (which was not submitted to the court of the first instance) to the appeal litigation. The limitation of new facts and evidence is, however, not absolute.

The two basic effects of the appeal are suspension and devolution. The suspense effect consists in the postponement of the legal force of the judgment. The latter effect consists of the transfer of the decision on the appeal to the Court of Appeal, and the court of first instance is fundamentally excluded from the decision-making on appeal. The role of the court of first instance in the appeal litigation is limited, and except for *autoremedura* (*see* Article 210a of CPC) this court cannot issue the decision on appeal.

The decision on appeal can be either on merit or procedural (the refusal of the appeal, the dismissal and the abolishment of the contested judgment or its confirmation). The possibility for the abolishment of the judgment was strictly limited by the amendment to the CPC in force since June 2005. This regulation constrains the appeal court to decide on the merit of the case and limits the possibility to abolish the judgment and to return the case to the court of first instance, which was generally considered as a cause of the delay in civil litigation.

§2. Cassation

134. The CPC regulates an extraordinary appeal as an extraordinary remedy, by which the judgments on the appeal might be contested. The extraordinary appeal is admissible on strictly regulated cases only because of its extraordinary nature (it perforates legal certainty). An extraordinary appeal is admissible when there is a need to unify the judicature (i.e., if a relevant legal question has not yet been subject to consideration by the Supreme Court or if it is decided in a different way by the courts), but the final consideration, if the extraordinary appeal will be admitted, belongs to the Supreme Court itself and the refusal of the extraordinary appeal has to be unanimous (by all the Judges – members of the bench).

The time limit for the extraordinary appeal is two months after the delivery of the judgments of the Court of Appeal. The entitled persons are the party and the subsidiary participant. This party has to be represented by an attorney (or by a notary) because serious legal questions are examined during the litigation on extraordinary appeal. Compulsory representation guarantees that the party will not sustain any injury because of a lack of legal knowledge.

135. A requirement of the extraordinary appeal is similar to the essentials of the appeal, i.e., general and special (the specification of the contested judgment, the extent of the extraordinary appeal, the reason and the evidence, which support the reason and the proposal). The extraordinary appeal due in time with all the essentials have only a devolutive effect, which means the decision on it will transfer to the Supreme Court of the Czech Republic.

The Supreme Court will examine the contested judgment fundamentally in the extension of the party's will, but it will cross this limit, for example, if there is a relation between the part of the predicate which was contested with the uncontested part (*see* Article 242 section 2 of CPC).

The extraordinary appeal will be examined and decided considering the principle of cassation. The contested judgment can be abolished, and independent of the reason for the abolishment, the Supreme Court will decide on the subsequent procedure (a new hearing of the case or the suspension of the litigation). The extraordinary appeal will be refused, if the contested judgment is considered to be correct. Besides these decisions on merit the Supreme Court can issue a procedural decision: to dismiss the extraordinary appeal (if it is delayed) or the litigation on the extraordinary appeal can be suspended (if the extraordinary appeal is deficient or if it is retracted). The implication of the cassation of the Supreme Court is that the court the decision of which was abolished (the Court of Appeal or therewith the judgment of the court of first instance) is bound to the legal opinion of the Supreme Court.

§3. Extraordinary Remedies

136. As of 2001, the CPC regulates two special extraordinary action claims, for the rectification of the judgment: the retrial and nullity plea.

A retrial is a remedy for the reopening of the case under circumstances that there are new substantial facts. The retrial is admissible if there are new facts, decisions or evidence that can be objectively submitted by the party within the primary litigation or there is a possibility to examine the evidence, which was not feasible within the primary litigation. The subjective time limit within which it can be claimed lasts three months and objective time limit lasts three years after the legal force of the decision. The court will at first decide if a retrial can be permitted and after permission, the court will hear a case again. The new decision will replace the primary decision on the matter.

The nullity plea is the remedy for the reparation of the defects of the litigation (lack of the procedural prerequisites or other substantial defects). The existence of these defects in the litigation brings up the need to overturn the decision irrespective if it was correct or not. Fundamentally, the nullity plea is admissible against judgments, which ends litigation. The time limit for the nullity plea is fundamentally three months after the delivery of the contested judgment. The court will abolish the contested judgment or the nullity plea will be dismissed.[6,7]

6. A. Winterová, A. Macková et al., *Civilní právo procesní* (*The Civil Procedure Law*) 9th edn. (Leges Praha a.s., 2018), pp. 513 and f.
7. A. Macková, *Opravné prostedky v novele OS provedené zákonem Č.30/2000 Sb.* (*The Post-Trial Remedies under Amedment No. 30/2000 Coll.*), Bulletin advokacie No. 8/2000.

Part V. Incidents

137. The parties perform their influence to the litigation and its subject by procedural acts (the action, the change of the action, withdrawal of the action, mutual action/counterclaim, the inclusion objection, the recognition of the debt and the settlement of the dispute). This influence is limited in non-adversary proceedings, but some exceptions are granted to the parties even in this kind of proceedings (*see* Articles 10, 13–15 of the Code on the Non-adversary Proceedings).

The action can be withdrawn in any stage of the litigation (*see* Article 96 of CPC), even if the court of first instance issued its decision (but if there is no legal force for the decision yet). The withdrawal of the action is admissible within the litigation either at the first instance or appeal litigation.

The withdrawal of the action can be made as a partial procedural act. In such a case, the court will partially suspend the litigation, and for the rest of the claim the litigation continues.

The withdrawal of the action is a reflection of the will of the party not to ask the court's protection of his/her rights anymore. The court will fundamentally suspend the litigation (if the withdrawal is made before the hearing or in divorce litigation). If there is no approval of the withdrawal by the opponent, the court will not accept the withdrawal. The defendant can have an interest that the court will decide the dispute by a judgment on merit. In such cases, the court will continue in the litigation after its decision that the withdrawal of the action by the plaintiff has no validity.

There is no reimbursement of costs in this case as the litigation was suspended due to withdrawal of the action.

138. The settlement of the dispute is a result of a procedural act of the parties (a conciliation), by which they express their common will to conclude the subject of the litigation or on its part (*see* Article 99 of CPC). The conclusion of the parties underscores the approval by the court and fully replaces the judgment. The approved settlement has the same legal effects as a judgment. The parties' conclusion can also cover the costs of the litigation.

The change of action is also admissible under Czech civil procedure law. The opponent must be informed about the change; therefore it must be delivered personally. The change of the action is acceptable only on the condition of the court's agreement. The court will not approve the change of the action; if the actual findings of the litigation cannot serve as a basis for litigation on the changed action (*see* Article 95 section 2 of CPC). This condition arises from the principle of procedural economy.

The parties have a relevant right to express an opinion on the person of the judge and lay judge which will hear their case (*see* Article 15a of CPC). The parties must obtain an instruction on this right. An impartial, independent and unbiased judge is a presupposition of a fair trial. This presupposition would be compromised if the judge is biased or if there is a reason to doubt he/she is unbiased with respect to his/her relation to the parties, the subject matter or the representatives of the parties. The previous decisions of a certain judge cannot be considered as the reasons to ascertain the impartiality of a judge.

To save the costs of litigation (the principle of the procedural economy), the law limits the right to object to whether or not a judge is unbiased. Such an objection can be presented at the latest in the first hearing in the presence of the judge or lay judge. If bias is determined later, the party is allowed to object against the judge up to fifteen days after such knowledge is determined.

An objection to a judge's impartiality will be examined by the immediate superior court, which will hear the opinion of the judge as well. The eliminated judge will be replaced by another judge, who is determined by the fixed court schedule.

The judge also may consider whether he/she is impartial or not. The president of the court will examine this issue. The president of the court will either consider the reason relevant or transfer this question to the superior court for further consideration.[8]

8. A. Macková, *Nezávislost soudc* (*The Independence of the Judge*) (UK Praha, 3. Vydání, 1998), p.37.

Part VI. Legal Aid and Legal Cost

Chapter 1. Legal Aid

139. The Czech Constitution guarantees the right to legal aid for everyone. Legal institutions and regulations regulate this right, the provision of which can waive the court fee, provide for legal representation by the court or the assignation of an attorney by the Bar.

The waiver of the court fee is granted under certain criteria by the law directly, or in certain cases of litigation, the court fee is waived as well. In certain circumstances, in litigation court fees can be waived if the person is in destitute circumstances (property and social) if the claim is not in effect at the same time (*see* Articles 30 and 138 of CPC). The examination of the conditions of the applicant is under judicial discretion and consideration. The waiving of court fees also provides for the possibility of free representation by an attorney (whose fee will be paid by the State) if it is necessary.

The law on attorneys entitles individual to ask the Czech Bar to provide him/her an attorney (legal aid system). This applies in such a case where no attorney wants to represent the applicant if there is a lack of means to pay an attorney's fee. If there are such refusals by attorneys or such a lack of means, the Czech Bar will select a certain attorney to provide legal service and at the same time lower the fee or decide that no fee will be fixed for such a case after examination of applicant's circumstances (property and social). The conditions of the applicants are subject to examination by the Czech Bar.

Besides this, there are free consultation days in the regional seats of the Czech Bar on a regular basis.

Legal Aid in Cross-Border Cases within the EU is based on Law 629/2004 Coll. which provides rules for Czech citizens in litigation abroad and foreigners in litigation in the Czech Republic as to how legal aid can be provided in those cases.

Chapter 2. Legal Costs

140. The costs of litigation cover cash expenses (including court fee), the costs of evidence, the attorney's fee and many other expenses. The amount the individual is charged is limited by legal regulation.

Act No. 549/1991 Coll. on Court Fees, as amended, regulates the court fee. The tariff rate is fixed, or it is determined as a percentage rate. In principle, the fee for the action is 5% of the recovered sum. If the subject of the action is non-monetary, the rate is fixed and governed by the law (*see* enclosure to the Act on Court Fees).

The attorney's fee is governed by the attorney's tariff (Ordinance of the Ministry of Justice No. 177/1996 Coll. as amended). The fee can be contractual or tariff. The contractual can be also a contingency fee or success fee. The contingency fee is regulated by the professional Code of Ethics. It has to be adequate to the subject and the complexity of the case. The success fee is admissible as an exception under special circumstances (social and property conditions of the client). As such, it serves in cases in which the person could not otherwise get legal services on a customary basis.

141. The rate of an attorney's fee is regulated in such cases in which there is no agreement between the attorney and his client (e.g., a compulsory criminal defence or a compulsory representation in civil litigation). The tariff establishes the rates for these cases.

The attorney is therefore obliged to inform his client, when they negotiate the contractual fee, that there is a regulation on costs (even when the client wins, he/she will bear the part of the costs without compensation – the difference between the contractual fee and the rate fixed by the special regulation).

The compensation of costs is dominated by the principles of success in litigation and the principle of culpability of the costs (the claimant is obliged to send the defendant a formal notice before the claim will be submitted to the court as a requisite which is followed by the court when adjudicating the compensation of costs). The fundamental difference rises from the adversary or non-adversary nature of the certain litigation.

The principle of the culpability of costs applies in both the kinds of litigation (adversary and non-adversary). The essence of the principle consists in compensation of costs borne by the person who is judged ultimately responsible. For example, a witness inflicted the costs because of his/her absence. The coincidence is relevant in the case of causing the inflexion of the costs by the party or his/her representatives.

Of fundamental relevance for the decision the court will make on the costs of litigation is based upon the principle of the success in the litigation. This factor will govern the complete compensation of costs in the case that there is a full success of a party. If the success of the party is partial, the court will split the costs. In exceptions, full compensation will be granted to the loser, if his/her behaviour did not cause the action (e.g., an action for notice to vacate a dwelling because the plaintiff needs the flat for his/her child).

Special competence of the court should be mentioned in this connection. The court is entitled to not grant compensation of the costs of litigation, although it pertains under the usual principles because the compensation would translate unreasonable demands.

The regulatory amendment brought up the possibility to consider compensation for the costs of litigation even in non-adversary litigation. The court is at the same time obliged to consider the circumstances of a certain case (the results of the litigation, the reason for the action, etc. – *see* Article 146 section 1 lit. a/).

The decision on the costs of litigation is in principle a part of the predicate of the judgments on merit. The court can decide on costs in a separate ruling. Some questions on the costs of the litigation can be decided however within the litigation (waiver, advance payment, etc.). The extent of the compensation is generally limited to the essential costs for the rational protection of the rights.[9]

9. A. Macková, *Právní pomoc advokát a její dostupnost* (*The Attorneys and Their Services*) (C.H. Beck, 2001); P. Bílek, L. Drápal et al., *Notáský ád a izení o dpozstalosti* (*The Notaries Rules and the Proceedings on Herritage*) (C.H. Beck, 2018).

Part VII. Evidence

Chapter 1. Burden of Proof

142. Historically, Czech civil procedure (like German, Austrian and generally continental) has been based on the distinction between factual findings and legal facts, both of which have to be available to the court for decision-making.

As regards factual findings (*question facti*), it principally holds that the parties in the proceedings have the obligation to present important facts (obligation to state the facts), and in connection with these facts they are obliged to propose the means to prove the same (obligation to suggest an evidence). These obligations are procedural ones, which mean that failing them will reflect on the outcome of the process. However, this is true in adversary proceedings only. In non-adversary proceedings, the court is obliged to find all the facts and the evidence which are requisites and essentials for the judgment.

As regards legal facts (legal knowledge), the old rule of written law applies to this issue: the court knows the law (*iura novit curia*). As far as the legal assessment of the matter is concerned, the parties have no procedural obligation to present their legal opinion.

143. The factual findings always represent individual and specific facts and actions. The obligation to state facts imposed on the parties is logical and necessary – the court itself does not know these facts and cannot establish them. However, the court must know the objective law and the core of its doing is to subordinate (subsume) the facts under a relevant legislation.

Consequences of the failure to meet the obligation to state the facts and the obligation to produce evidence to prove these facts differ in adversary and non-adversary proceedings.

144. In the adversary proceedings, the obligation to state facts is linked with the burden of allegation, and the obligation to evidence is linked to the burden of proof. In principle then, if a party fails to meet its obligation to state the facts, it has failed to bear the burden of allegation, and if it fails to meet its obligation to evidence, it has failed to bear the burden of proof. Both failures result in the loss of the case. (Similarly, the defendant bears the burden of fact and burden of proof in connection with his defence against the litigation). The issue of the burden of proof (*onus probandi*) is one that comes to play in practice more often. However, the burden of proof is not absolute. In principle, it is true that he/she who states facts must prove the facts. In compliance with Article 120 paragraph 2 of the Code of Civil Procedure, the court may admit other evidence than that proposed by the parties in cases when it appears needed in connection with establishing the facts and when the file of the case contains it. Naturally, the court must learn about such evidence in a different way than from the motions of the parties, but it has no obligation (and no power) to investigate.

In non-adversary proceedings, the parties also have the duty to state facts and the duty to prove facts, but these obligations are not linked to the burden of allegation and burden of proof. In these proceedings, the court is obliged to admit other evidence than that proposed by the parties (Article 21 of the Code on the Non-adversary Proceedings).

145. Evidence is assessed on the basis of a discretionary principle which relies on the individual perception of the value of the evidence by the judge. The only legal obligation of the judge is to assess each piece of evidence individually and all of them in their entirety and with mutual links (free evaluation of the evidence principle). Further, the court must take into account all facts which were ascertained during the hearing including statements by the parties (Article 132 of the Code of Civil Procedure). All the considerations must be outlined in the justification of the judgment (in it is reasoning).

Because the assessment of evidence is within the discretion and the consideration of the judge, it must not be changed during the appeal in principle (the appellate judge must not assess the same evidence in a different manner), unless the appellate court decides to take evidence anew. Then it can use its discretionary power to assess it.

146. There is only one exception when it comes to the discretionary assessment of evidence and that pertains to public documents (documents with the public faith). Public documents include documents issued by courts or other government bodies within the scope of their powers and documents which are declared public by law (such as notary deeds and deeds of court executors). Public documents, if genuine, are considered to be a true statement or order of that body which issued the document. Further, public documents confirm as true whatever they certify unless proved untrue (Article 134 of the Code of Civil Procedure). Public documents have a greater power of proof as evidence when compared with private documents.

147. Only facts which are relevant for the application of law are subject to evidence taking. Some facts, although relevant, do not have to be proved and the court deems them proved. These facts include:

- facts on which both parties to the adversary proceedings agree;
- facts notoriously known;
- facts known to the court from its own activity (e.g., from other cases in its files); and
- facts which are considered by law to be a legal assumption (*praesumptio*), unless the opposite arises from the proceedings.

If the value of the claim is difficult or impossible to establish, the court has the discretion to determine the value of the claim (for instance, a claim for indemnification for damage).

148. The law is not subject to evidence taking. This rule applies to legal regulations (constitutional Acts, laws, government decrees and implementing regulations) which were published or at least announced in the official Collection of Laws and Collection of the International Treaties of the Czech Republic. Published international treaties ratified by the Parliament and binding for the Czech Republic are an inherent part of the legal order and prevail over domestic laws (Article 10 of the Constitution of the Czech Republic). The court has the obligation to be familiar with international law. However, domestic law of other countries is subject to evidence taking.

Chapter 2. Admissibility of Evidence

149. The concept of admissibility of evidence, as set out in the Introductory provisions of the Code of Civil Procedure, Chapter II regarding evidence, is in keeping with the principle of discretionary powers of the court (Article 125 of the Code of Civil Procedure). The provision lays down: All means by which a true state (circumstances) of a case may be ascertained may be used as evidence.

It is the judge who decides without any restrictions about the admissibility of the proposed means of evidence. The only guiding consideration is whether the proposed evidence may help establish facts in a given case. If the manner in which a particular means of evidence is taken is not prescribed, the court shall determine it. Theoretically, therefore, and it has already been adjudicated by the Supreme Court, such means of evidence which are not provided for by law are admissible, including an affidavit and pretrial discovery documents (Decision/No. 26/1987, Collection of Decisions).

Chapter 3. Administration of Evidence

§1. Forced Production of Documents

150. The means of evidence which are enumerated in the Code of Civil Procedure are those that are typically and most often used:

- questioning of witnesses;
- expert opinion;
- reports and statements of authorities and individuals;
- notary deeds and deeds of court executors;
- on-the-spot examination; and
- questioning of the parties.

151. Regarding documents (Article 129 of CPC): Documents as means of evidence are either public documents – documents with the public faith (for definition and power – *see* hereinabove) – or private documents. Most often, notary deeds are mentioned. These are considered by respective laws to be public documents. Article 6 of the Notarial Rules designates as public documents notary deeds, original copies thereof, extracts from notary deeds and certification deeds (certification of copies or signatures). Similarly, Article 79 of the Rules of Execution designate as a public document the deed through which the party has taken on the obligation to perform under it and has agreed that in case of failure to perform, the document itself will serve as an execution title.

Following section 129 of CPC, the court may order anyone to submit a needed object or document to the court (the violation of this order is under financial penalty (maximum CZK 50.00 – ca. EUR 2000)). The problematic and controversial question if such an order may be imposed on the parties (which means losing the case) was answered by the Supreme Court: it can be imposed but financial penalty punishment only if not followed.

§2. Deposition of Witnesses

152. Regarding questioning of witnesses (Article 126 of CPC): Every individual who is not a party in the proceedings has the legal obligation to testify. He/she must appear when summoned, tell the truth about what he/she heard or saw or otherwise perceived and not withhold anything. This obligation is not tied to any legal age. A person lacking procedural capacity or a person who may be considered biased may still be questioned as witnesses.

153. A failure to appear before the court may result in the witness being brought before the court and/or fined up to CZK 50,000 (ca. EUR 2,000). A witness may be criminally charged for untrue or incomplete testimony, i.e., for perjury. The witness must be instructed by the court in all his/her rights and duties prior to the questioning.

154. A witness has the right to refuse testimony only if by the testimony he/she would expose himself or herself, or persons close to him, to the risk of criminal prosecution. However, he/she must appear and explain the reasons for such refusal. The court shall decide whether a refusal to testify is warranted or not. Secrecy and confidentiality issues are another matter – *see* below. The witness is entitled to a witness' fee, which is a reimbursement of cost and lost wage. The fee is paid by the court, but it is included in the costs of the proceedings; the costs are recovered from the parties according to the decision of the court. In adversary proceedings, the allocation of costs depends on the outcome of the case.

§3. Deposition of Parties Themselves

155. Regarding questioning of the parties (Article 131 of CPC): In the adversary proceedings, questioning of the parties are only of an auxiliary value; in other words, parties are questioned only when and if the fact cannot be proved otherwise and subject to consent of the party to be questioned. In non-adversary proceedings, no such limitations apply, and the questioning of the parties is widely admissible.

§4. Expert Evidence

156. Regarding the expert opinion (Article 127 of CPC): If a judicial decision depends on the evaluation of facts for which expert knowledge is required, the court shall appoint an expert. The parties have the right to speak to the choice of the expert, in particular in connection with a possible bias. The expert is chosen from the official list administered by the Ministry of Justice. The same evidence value is given to the expert opinion provided by any of the parties if it includes the expert clause and declaration on his or her neutrality (*see* section 127a of CPC). Court-certified translators have a similar position. Unlike a witness, the expert must not be biased. If the expert opinion was made upon request of a party, it might be as well used, provided that it contains the same legal requisites as the expert opinion issued upon request of the court.

157. The expert should address the issue in question orally, most often; however, he may also be asked to deliver a written opinion. Several experts may be appointed and submit a joint opinion. An expert opinion may also be re-examined by another expert, a scientific institute or another institution if there are reasons to do so. The appointed expert has no coercive powers. If cooperation of parties is needed, in the form of a medical examination, blood tests, etc., the court shall order the parties to do so. An expert (or translator) is entitled to the expert's fee comprised of out-of-pocket expenses and remuneration. The fee is paid by the court, but it is included in the costs of the proceedings; the costs are recovered from the parties according to the decision of the court. In adversary proceedings, the allocation of costs depends on the outcome of the case. In the course of the proceedings, the parties may be asked to advance a deposit to the court to cover the cost of evidence taking (including fees to witnesses and experts).

Instead of hearing the expert, which is a priority, the court may accept with a written opinion or with an expert statement.

§5. Affidavit

158. There is no regulation of the affidavit in the CPC in the Czech Republic.

§6. Reports of Authorities and Individuals

159. Regarding reports and statements of authorities and individuals (Article 128 of CPC): Everybody is obliged to communicate to the court, free of charge, facts which are important for the proceedings and the judicial decision. Individuals may refuse to communicate to the court on the same grounds as witnesses (*see* above). Free-of-charge communication of important facts may be linked to the obligation to produce a document needed as evidence or an item to be examined as evidence. A person meeting his/her obligation to produce documents is entitled to the same reimbursement as a witness.

§7. Spot Examination

160. Regarding the on-the-spot examination (Article 130 of CPC): The examination of an object which can be brought to the court shall be done at one of its sessions. Otherwise, the examination shall be carried out on the spot. In both cases, a written report is drafted.

§8. Inspection by Judge

161. Taking of evidence is in the hands of judges, not the parties or their legal counsels. The party's obligation to prove is fulfilled when the party proposes certain evidence and clearly and precisely designates it. Those rules fully apply in the adversary proceedings.

In non-adversary proceeding, the principle of investigation applies. In non-adversary proceedings, the parties also have the duty to state facts and the duty to prove facts, but these obligations are not linked to the burden of allegation and burden of proof. In these proceedings, the court is obliged to admit other evidence than that proposed by the parties (Article 21 of the Code on the Non-adversary Proceedings) for to make the factual findings as necessary for to apply the law.

The obligation of the court is to solicit evidence by summons, requests for public documents, etc. Only in case of documents which the claimant proposes as evidence and which are in his possession, the claimant is obliged to attach them to the claim.

162. In principle, evidence is to be taken during the court hearing. Only in exceptional and justified cases and upon request, evidence may be presented to the court or the judge outside of the hearing. Parties, however, have the right to be present and the outcome of such presentation must be then communicated orally during the hearing.[10]

The court must hear evidence in keeping with the protection of classified information and must respect the confidentiality obligation unless the witness is relieved from the confidentiality duty by the respective authority.[11]

Evidence performance at the oral hearing is controlled by the court. Respective provisions of the Code of Civil Procedure (Articles 126 through 131 of CPC) specify how various types of evidence are to be handled. (For instance, before the questioning of the witness, any circumstances which might affect his credibility are to be ascertained. The witness is also advised and instructed in his/her rights and duties and criminal consequences of perjury. Only thereafter may questions be asked, first by the presiding judge and then by members of the bench and with the presiding judge's consent, their attorneys and experts or parties may then ask questions. In the case of documents, the presiding judge reads documentary evidence out loud or informs about its content).

10. L. David et al., Čanský soudní ád, Wolters Kluwer, 2009, p. 567.
11. A. Winterova, A. Macková et al., *Civilní právo procesní* (*The Civil Procedure Law*) 9th edn. (Leges, a.s., 2018), p. 221.

Part VIII. Particular Proceedings

Chapter 1. Summary Proceedings with Documentary Evidence

163. The CPC regulates the summary proceedings for the recovery of the pecuniary sum (*see* Articles 172–174 of CPC) and the active debts from the bills of exchange and cheques. In these special litigations, the court decides by special form of decision – payment order (bill of exchange payment order or cheque payment order).

There is a special procedure for electronic payment order, which is limited for claims under CZK 1,000,000 (ca. EUR 38,400). Such a claim is admissible in electronic form with secured electronic signature only (*see* Article 174a of CPC).

The litigation on the active pecuniary debt can proceed even if there is no such a proposal of the plaintiff. The prerequisites of such a procedure are:

- the pecuniary nature of the debt; and
- the statements of the plaintiff should support the claim.

Under the given conditions, the judge is entitled to decide without hearing and to decide the defendant is obliged to pay the debt and the costs within the time limit of fifteen days after the delivery of the payment order.

The procedural defence of the defendant consists in the possibility to contest the payment order by protest. The consequence of the protest is the abolishment of the payment order and the continuing of litigation with hearing.

The payment order cannot be issued if the case should be decided by the bench of judges, if the payment order should be delivered abroad or if there is no knowledge about the residence of the defendant. There is no limit concerning the amount of the sum, which can be subject of the payment order. The active debts, however, have to be supported by the plaintiff's relevant statements.

164. The summary proceedings on cheques and bills of exchange are its other form. In these cases, there must be a special proposal of the plaintiff, the court should issue the payment order. The plaintiff has to submit the original cheque or original bill of exchange, which is not doubtful. The competent court for the issuing of the payment order is the regional court (*see* Article 9 paragraph 3, lit. j/CPC). The local competent court is given to be choice (the common court of the defendant or the court in which region is the place of the payment).

Regulation (EC) No. 1896/2006 of the European Parliament and of the Council of 12 December 2006 creating a European order for payment procedure was implemented into Czech civil procedure (*see* Article 174b of CPC).

The law on cheques and bill of exchanges (No. 191/1950 Coll.) limits the defence of the defendant. The defendant can contest the payment order by a counter-plea within the time limit of fifteen days, which must be argued in the same time limit.

The counter-plea has other effects compared to protest against the general payment order. There is no direct abolishment of the payment order due to counter-plea. The counter-plea will be discussed on hearing. After the hearing, the court decides if the cheque payment order or the bill of exchange payment order will be abolished (partially abolished) or not. The decision on the counter-plea can be contested by an appeal.

Chapter 2. Family Matters

165. The doctrinal difference between the adversary and non-adversary litigation is consequentially projected to the legal system of the Czech Republic since 2013 when the Law No. 292/2013 Coll. on non-adversary (special) proceeding was adopted. The previous united regulation, of both types of proceedings (adversary and non-adversary proceeding) in the CPC, was a residuum of the concept of unification of litigation, which had dominated the doctrine of the civil procedure from the 1950s till the fundamental changes after 1989.

After the restitution of the traditional principles of private law (expressed by the new Civil Code – Law No. 89/2012 Coll. which is in effect since 1 January 2014), the traditional principles of the continental contradictory procedure (such as the principle of contradictory and the disposition principle) were reflected to the protection of the rights. The court, however, decides in civil litigation other matters then only in disputes in private law. Those non-adversary proceedings are thus regulated by (hereinabove mentioned) special law. This regulation applies exclusively for enumerated proceedings (*see* Article 2 of the Code on the Non-adversarial Proceedings). The litigation on such matters is dominated by completely different principles (such as the inquisitorial principle and the 'ex officio' principle) compared to adversarial proceedings.

Such matters are the issues on legacy heritage, the issues of the minors, the issues on adults under the special court's protection (litigation on the establishment of a guardian, the detection litigation, etc.), the litigation on the legal status of a natural person (litigation on legal capacity, litigation on presumption on death), litigation on legal status of corporations (litigation on the register of companies), matrimonial and other family law matters (like divorce, adoptions, paternity) and many others.

It means the litigation on family matters and matters of minors is thus performed under different legal regimes then the typical contradictory dispute between claimant and defendant in adversarial proceedings. The regime of the non-adversary litigation is laid down under the Code of Non-adversary Proceeding No. 292/2013 Coll. for matters on upbringing and sustenance of minors, contact between the child and parents or grandparents and brothers and sisters, custody for the child to the entitled person, the granting, the limitation or exoneration of the responsibility of parents, the tutorship, the approval of relevant legal acts of the minor, the prolongation of the upbringing in an institution after full age, the permission to end a marriage, the determination of an agreement of the parents that adoption is unavoidable, etc.

All the above-mentioned matters are treated in litigation dominated by the inquisitorial principle and the 'ex officio' principle, which reflects the public interest in its authoritative decision with the eventual participation of the public prosecutor (*see* Article 35 of CPC and Article 8 of the Code on Non-adversary Proceedings). The dissimilarity of the non-adversary litigation consists also in the nature of the appeal, which is admitted as a full appeal, which allows the parties to submit new facts and evidence to the appeal litigation.[12]

12. A. Winterová, A. Macková et al., *Civilní procesní právo* (*The Civil Procedure Law*) 9th edn. (Leges Praha a.s., 2018), pp. 438 and f.

Part IX. Seizure for Security and Enforcement of Judgment

Chapter 1. Seizure for Security

§1. Proceedings

166. If there is original of the cheque or the bill of exchange, which is not doubtful and other documents which entitled the plaintiff and if there is at the same time such a proposal by the plaintiff, the court will issue the special payment order. The payment order is a command to pay the debt and the costs.

§2. Judicial Review

167. The legal regulation on litigation on cheques and the bills of exchange reflects its regulation (No. 191/1950 Coll.). The procedure by which the issued payment order can be contested reflects the mentioned regulation also. The counter-plea against the payment order is the only defence, which can be exercised in the determined time limit (fifteen days). The later counter-plea will not be considered (the concentration of the counter-plea). The decision on the counter-plea can be contested by the appeal.

Chapter 2. Enforcement of Judgments

§1. Enforcement of Domestic Judgments

I. Proceedings

168. The enforcement of the judgment can be performed by the court. The creditor can also use the services of the executor (*see* Law No. 120/2001 Coll.), which nowadays means an alternative procedure for the enforcement of the judgments for the creditors. Law on executors was the subject of wide revision and amendments. The role of the executors in the enforcement of the judgments is stronger, and courts enforce just some of the judgments exclusive (like the judgments on relations to minors, a domestic violence an eviction with alternative housing or similar cases).

The legal regulation on the court's enforcement of judgments is included in Part VI of the CPC (Articles 251–351a of CPC).

The opening of this special litigation is dominated by the disposition principle. The entitled person to open this litigation is the creditor, whose claim is entitled by the title. The title designates who will be the entitled party and who will be the obliged person in the executory litigation. The entitled person fundamentally chooses the way of the execution. If the debts consist of non-pecuniary behaviour, the means of the execution is predetermined by the title (but if the execution is performed by the court executor, not by the court, the entitled party is not obliged to choose the way how the debt should be enforced, because it is a task of the court executor, who will accomplish easily the information on the debtor property).

The action on execution must be coupled with the copy of the title which should be performed. The title is the judgment of the court (lawful) or another type of decision, which are enumerated by the CPC.

169. The ways of the execution are enumerated strictly in CPC:

(1) Pecuniary debts:
   (a) wage deduction;
   (b) adjudgment of receivable;
   (c) an order for payment (for non-concrete bank);
   (d) sale of movable or immovable objects; and
   (e) forced administration (trust) of immovable objects or enterprise; and
   (f) the court executor can also suspend the driving licence of the debtor, where there is his/her debt in alimony (for minor).
   (g) judicial mortgage.
(2) Non-pecuniary obligation:
   (a) eviction-alternative housing;
   (b) removal of an object;
   (c) distribution of the jointly owned object; and
   (d) performance of work or services.

The special means of execution are regulated for the enforcement of judgments on the upbringing of minors and\contact with them and the judgments on domestic violence.

170. The execution is dominated by the principle of the adequacy of the debts and the means of execution.

Before the execution is declared, the court may call the obliged party to declare on his/her property (*see* Article 260a of CPC). The nature of the judicial declaration on property is to get the information on the property of the obliged party, and every creditor (whose debt is supported by the lawful decision) can see the court record with such a declaration of the obliged party. After such information is available to the creditor, he/she may choose the reasonable and adequate way of execution.

The court performance of the title is handled by the district courts. The local competent court is in principle the court in which district the obliged person has residency or seat. The parties to the litigation on execution are, besides the entitled person and the obliged person, the spouse of the obliged person, if there is common ownership between husband and wife.

The execution has, in principle, two stages. The first stage consists of the declaration of execution. If this decision (on the declaration of the execution) is lawful (legal force), the second stage – the performance of the execution – follows without any further special creditor motion.

The execution can be postponed only under the special circumstances (primarily social relations). The execution can be suspended as well if there is a relevant impediment (e.g., a defect of the executory title). The fundamental completion of the execution should consist of the satisfaction of debts.

II. Judicial Review

171. The obliged person is within the execution protected directly by the law. The law determines which objects are not the subject of the execution or in the case of a deduction of wages an amount of money for the obliged person and his/her family is protected. This protection does not depend on the will of the obliged party. Besides this, there are legal remedies, which can be applied by the obliged person (such as an appeal, the proposal for the postponement or suspension of the execution). The same applies to third parties (e.g., the spouse of the debtor), who are entitled to use a special procedural remedy to protect their rights (in the case their property is unlawfully involved into the debtor property).

The regional court will hear the appeal against the declaration of the execution. The obliged person can also claim a special action on the negation of the amount of the debt, its existence or validity. The execution may involve the rights of third parties. These persons (e.g., the spouse of the obliged party) are entitled to claim for exclusion of their property from the execution.

§2. Recognition and Enforcement of Foreign Judgments

I. Rules Applicable in the Absence of a Treaty

172. EU Regulation No. 1215/2012 on Civil Jurisdiction and the Recognition and Enforcement of a judgment in civil and commercial matters applies in relations between the Member States of the EU.

The EU Regulation No. 805/2004 on European Executory Title for the undisputed claims, which applies from October 2005, contributes to the free movement of the Judgments. The decision, which is verified as European Executory Title, will be recognized and executed in other Member State, and it has the nature of the domestic judgment (*see* Article 353 of CPC).

The regulation implicated in the Act on IPLP applies if there is no treaty.

II. International Treaties

173. The Czech Constitution expresses the pre-eminence of international treaties over the domestic law (*see* Article 10 and Article 95 section 1 of the Constitution). The legal relations with foreign elements are regulated by the Law No. 91/2012 Coll. on International Civil Law and International Procedure.

The judgments are issued in the name of the State. Therefore, the recognition and the enforcement of judgments are bound to a great many conditions, expressed in multilateral or bilateral international treaties (the treaties on international justice cooperation or special treaties on recognition and enforcement of a judgment). The regulation in the Act on IPLP applies if there is no such a treaty or EU regulation (e.g., Regulation EC No. 1215/2012, Regulation EC No. 650/2012, Regulation EC No. 2201/2003, Regulation EC No. 848/2015, Regulation EC No. 805/2004, Regulation No. 1896/2006, Regulation EC No. 861/2007 and Regulation No. 1347/2000).

The recognition of the judgment means it will have the same effects as a judgment of a Czech court. The enforcement of the judgment means the obliged person will be forced to address a duty specified in a foreign judgment.

All the hereinabove mentioned regulations reflect the fact that the foreign judgment is a judgment of the justice system of the foreign state.

A. *Brussels Convention*

174. One of the most relevant international treaties on the recognition and enforcement of the foreign judgments – pursuant to its frequency of application – is the Brussels Convention on Jurisdiction and Enforcement of Judgments on Civil and Commercial Matters, signed on 27 September 1968.

As far as EU relations are concerned, the Convention was in its extent replaced by EU Regulation No. 1215/2012, on Civil Jurisdiction and Recognition and Enforcement of Judgments in Civil and Commercial Matters (Brussels I. bis).

B. Lugano Convention

175. The Lugano Convention was agreed at Lugano in 1988 for the (EFTA – European Free Trade Association) Member States, whose access to the Brussels Convention was limited. Some of the Member States of the EFTA have since become Member States of the EU. The relevancy of the Lugano Convention is therefore becoming weaker.

Part X. Arbitration

Chapter 1. Arbitrability

176. Everyone has his/her constitutional right to court protection of rights (*see* Article 36, paragraph 1 of Bill/Charter of Fundamental Rights and Freedoms, Act. No. 2/1993 Coll. as amended and Article 1 of CPC, which regulates the procedure of the court and parties of the civil litigation so that the protection of the rights and rightful interest would be fully vested).

The protection of the rights and rightful interests is the fundamental task of the courts, which should be independent and impartial, and the parties have a mutually equivalent position in the law. The courts are entitled to decide these disputes authoritatively. The court's protection of rights is the fundamental principle of the rule of law.

The Bill/Charter of Fundamental Rights and Freedoms, however, also allows different legal protection (*see* Article 36, paragraph 1: 'Everyone is entitled to demand in determined procedure at the independent and impartial court or at the determined cases at the different organ.').

The Bill of Fundamental Rights and Freedoms also expresses the principle of the legal judge (Article 38 paragraph 1: 'No one can be subducted from his/her legal judge.'). This principle provides a guarantee that cases should not be purposefully changed between judges at anybody's will. The principle of the legal judge ensures that the law (equal and notorious) determines the rules for the assignment of cases to an appropriate judge (the Court Schedule). The establishment of the courts and their personal staffing cannot be incidental.

177. The European Court of Human Rights in Strasbourg declared in case Campbell Fell (1984) that 'it must not be the court body, integrated to the court system'. Other tribunals, which are concerned with individual rights must be independent (in conformity with the right to a fair trial). The rules on its functioning subsume the guarantee of independence, such as the means of appointment and lack of bias.

The methods of alternative disputes resolution in the Czech Republic are arbitration, mediation and consumer dispute resolution (by the Czech Commercial Inspection, Energetic Regulatory Authority, Czech Telecommunication Authority, Czech Bar, Association of the Czech Consumers, Financial Arbiter or Ombudsman of the Czech Insurance Association).

178. In relation with international arbitration, the Czech court considers the admissibility of the arbitration agreement under Czech law (i.e., under the Act on Arbitration and the Enforcement of the Arbitral Awards).

If the arbitration award should be issued in the Czech Republic, the essential of the arbitration agreement has to be considered under the Czech law as well. The form of the arbitration award is determined by the law, which determines other essentials of the arbitration agreement. The essentials, however, can be satisfied under the law of the country in which the arbitration agreement was concluded.

Chapter 2. Arbitration Agreement and Party Autonomy

179. Arbitration is the procedure mutually (voluntarily) agreed upon to reach an authoritative decision on a dispute between parties. It is a special kind of civil procedure; an arbitral award might be enforced such as a judgment of the court. The arbitration award has the same effects as a court judgment. The difference between civil litigation and arbitration consists in the special nature of the persons who resolve the disputes. These individuals are private persons. Another difference between these two procedures lies in the equity, which is the principle under which the dispute is decided upon. The equity principle, however, cannot be in violation of the peremptory rules. The role of an impartial third person belongs in arbitration to the one or more arbiters.

180. Arbitration is not the only alternative dispute resolution method regulated by the Czech legal system at present. Mediation became a legally confirmed alternative method as well by the adoption of a new Act on Mediation No. 202/2012 Coll. Regulation of arbitration is in Act No. 216/1994 Coll. as amended, on Arbitration and the Enforcement of the Arbitral Awards.

181. The parties can choose arbitration for property disputes, which otherwise fall under the jurisdiction of general courts. A prerequisite for arbitration is an arbitration agreement. The arbitration agreement must be written, and it may be agreed as an agreement on arbiter(s) or as an arbitration clause (*see* Article 2 Act on Arbitration and Enforcement of the Arbitral Awards). The agreement on arbiter(s) is an agreement, which is concluded after the dispute has arisen, and it covers only one specific dispute. The arbitration clause is, on the contrary, an agreement that all the disputes between the agreed parties which could arise in future on a contract to which the arbitration clause is connected are submitted to the arbiters, in lieu of the court. The consumer protection matters may not be a subject of the arbitration since December 2016 in the Czech Republic.

Fundamentally, the extent of the arbitration agreement covers the rights arising from certain legal relationships and rights which are connected to these rights. The parties may however modify this to an extent.

The court examines the existence of the arbitration agreement only if there is the objection by the defendant at the first procedural act in civil litigation. If the court finds that there is an arbitration agreement, it will be considered as an impediment to the continuing of civil litigation and the court must suspend it (*see* Article 106 of CPC). If there is a declaration by the parties that they do not insist in their arbitration agreement, the court will decide their dispute. The court will decide the dispute if the dispute can be the subject of the arbitration agreement, if the arbitration agreement is not valid or it does not exist or if the competence of the arbiters was determined to be inadmissible or if the arbitration court refused to hear the case.

The arbitration agreement has to be compulsorily written, and it obliges the successors of the parties of the agreement, if not specified otherwise.

Chapter 3. The Composition of Arbitral Tribunal

182. The arbitration body can be either one or more arbiters (ad hoc arbitration) or the permanent court of arbitration, which might be established by the law only (there are three of these permanent arbitration courts – *see* Part I, §1). An arbiter can be an appointed Czech citizen or foreigner, fully legally capable, unbiased who accepted the appointment. A Czech citizen who acts as an arbiter must be an adult, fully legally capable and have no legal restrictions; for example, justices of the Constitutional Court, judges of the general courts and public prosecutors cannot be arbiters. A foreigner must be fully legally capable under the law of the domicile of his/her country or have full legal capacity under the Czech law.

There is no obligation to adopt the function of the arbiter. If an individual accepts the position, he/she must perform the role in conformity with the legal order.

Acceptance of the function must be in writing. To resign from the function of the arbiter is possible only under relevant circumstances or with the agreement of the parties.

The arbiters are bound by secrecy on all the facts connected with their function. Arbiters can be relieved of the vow of secrecy by the parties. In some relevant cases, the president of the district court (in the residence of the arbiter) will decide on this issue, when the parties concerned do not decide on the matter.

The question of how many arbiters should decide a certain dispute is decided upon by the concerned parties. If the case belongs to the competency of the permanent court of arbitration, the number of the arbiters will be determined by the rules of that court.

The arbiters can be selected as soon as the dispute has been raised. In principle, in such a case rule applies under which, after the selection of one arbiter by one party, and after the announcement of this, there is a time limit of thirty days for the second party. If there is no selection of an arbiter within the time limit, the arbiter will be selected by the court under the proposal of the first party who selected an arbiter. There is a subsequent thirty-day time limit for the selection of the presiding arbiter. The court will determine the presiding arbiter (under the proposal of any party or the selected arbiter) if there is no such selection.

To maintain impartiality, arbiters are obliged to declare to the parties any facts which would raise doubt about their lack of bias. If there is an abdication of an arbiter or if there is another impediment, a subsequent procedure subordinates to the rules expressed in the arbitration agreement. If there is no such rule, the appointment of a new arbiter will be made by the court. The court addresses the need for impartiality and assures independent decision-making.

The arbiter is obliged to abdicate if there is the reason to do so subsequently. If the arbiter does not abdicate, the arbitration agreement or the court will decide how to proceed.

183. The permanent court of arbitration might be established by the law only (*see* Article 13 of the Act No. 216/1994 Coll. as amended, on Arbitration and the Enforcement of the Arbitral Awards). The permanent courts are entitled to issue its regulations, which must be published in the official Commercial Reports. These rules can regulate the appointment of arbiters, the number of arbiters and can connect the appointment of arbiters assigned to the list of arbiters at the permanent court. There can also be a regulation on litigation and decision-making and other issues, connected with the activity of the permanent court including a rule on compensation of costs and the arbiter's fee (*see* www. soud.cz).

If the parties agree on the competency of the permanent court of arbitration and there is no other rule in the agreement, then the parties have to accept the regulations of this permanent court valid at the time of the opening of the arbitration.

The arbitration is opened from the day the action is delivered to the permanent arbitration court or to the arbiter (presiding arbiter or any other arbiter, if the presiding arbiter was not determined at that time).

Chapter 4. Interim Measures and Preliminary Awards

184. An interim measure might be issued by the court at the behest of one party if there is a doubt on the successful future execution of the arbitration award. The preliminary award (measure) is not accepted by the practice of courts (*see* www.nsoud.cz).

Chapter 5. Conduct of Arbitral Proceeding

185. The arbiters are entitled to examine their competency, and they can decide on their incompetence. The parties also can question the competence of the arbiters (the arbitrability of the matter), the validity of the arbitration agreement, the existence of the arbitration agreement or its expiration at the first legal act in arbitration, at the latest (except for an objection the arbitration agreement can be concluded in this matter).

The place of the arbitration is governed by a mutually agreed upon decision of the parties. In the event of the no such a decision, the arbiters will determine the place of the arbitration while considering the rightful interests of the parties.

The position of the parties of the arbitration is equal, and their rights are mutually guaranteed.

The arbitration agreement usually regulates the method by which a decision is reached and the procedural rules and the substantive law under which the arbiters have to consider when resolving the dispute (or it is stipulated in rules which are a part/enclosure of the arbitration agreement). In a case where there are no such rules, the arbiters are entitled to handle the case in a proper and adequate way. The arbitration should not be uselessly formal. Both parties should be granted the same possibility to make their claims and demands due to factual respect of the case.

The arbitration is not public, and in principle it is oral (if there is no other settlement agreed by parties). The examination of witnesses and experts or parties can be performed only if the examined person voluntarily appears and testifies. This voluntary action principally applies to other evidence as well. The arbiters should urge the parties to conclude the settlement.

The arbitration award is made under substantive law which is relevant to the dispute. The arbiters are entitled by the parties to resolve the dispute on the equity principle if there is such an explicit authorization by the parties.

The role of the court within an arbitration is to perform the legal procedures, which cannot be performed by the arbiters if there is such a request of the arbiters. The court's expenses are compensated by permanent court of arbitration or by the arbiters.

The court may issue, during the arbitration, a preliminary measure at the behest of one party, if there is a doubt on the successful future execution of the arbitration award.

The CPC applies to the arbitration litigation appropriately (supportively), if there is no different rule in the Act on Arbitration and Enforcement of Arbitral Awards.

Chapter 6. Arbitral Award

186. The arbitration usually finishes by a decision on the merit of the case (the arbitration award) or by the ruling (without a decision on merit). The arbitration award must be decided by a majority of votes, must be written and signed by at least a majority of arbiters. The reasoning of the award must be clear and explicit, but the presence of the reasoning at the award is under the parties' will.

The arbitration award, which is not subject to review, or if the time limit within which the proposal for review can be submitted, is in legal force after it is delivered. Such an award has the same effects as a judgment, including enforceability.

Arbitration is, in principle, for one instance only. The parties, however, can settle for a review of the award by other arbiters. The proposal for review has to be submitted within a thirty-day time limit after delivery of the award.

The review of the award is part of the original arbitration and it is, in principle, under the same legal regulation.

Chapter 7. Recourse Against Arbitral Award

187. The role of the general courts in arbitration is broad. One of its competencies is to abolish the issued award; therefore, there is a duty to record the issued awards.

The arbiters are obliged to hand over the issued awards (with indicated legal force and documents which explain the course of the arbitration) within a thirty-day time limit to the court (in which district it was issued). The permanent courts of arbitration are obliged to record the awards (with indicated legal force and documents which explain the course of the arbitration) for twenty years after enforcement. The parties are entitled to see the recorded documents and to make copies.

The proposal for the abolishment of the award by the court is admissible within a three-month time limit (after the delivery of award). There is no suspension of the enforceability of the award due to a proposal for the abolishment of the award. The enforceability of the award can be suspended under the special proposal of the defendant if there is a risk of serious damage.

The court will abolish the award if:

(a) it was issued in the matter in which no valid arbitration agreement can be concluded;
(b) the arbitration agreement is non-valid, was cancelled or does not cover the matter;
(c) the matter was decided by the arbiter who was not selected properly, or there was a lack of his capacity;
(d) the award was not issued by the majority of the arbiters;
(e) the party was not granted the possibility to present a case;
(f) the arbitration award was a command to perform an act which is not allowed under Czech law;
(g) the arbitration award was issued in contradiction to moral rules or public order; and
(h) there are reasons for a retrial (the same way as under the CPC – *see* Article 228 of CPC).

The court will refuse the proposal for the abolishment of the award if it is supported by the reason *abo*ve-mentioned (b) and (c) and if the party did not make such an objection during the original arbitration litigation.

After the abolishment of the award due to reason (a) or (b) or (g) or (h) hereinabove mentioned, the court will continue in litigation if there is such a proposal of the party. In other cases, the arbitration agreement will stay valid after the abolishment of the award.

The arbiters, who decided in the original arbitration (abolished under (c)), are excluded in the new arbitration. The arbiters for the new arbitration will be appointed under the regime determined in the agreement or under the law. The parties are, however, entitled to conclude an agreement on this issue.

The arbitration agreement will stay valid after the abolishment of the award (except cases (a) and (b)).

Chapter 8. Recognition and Enforcement of Awards

§1. Recognition and Enforcement of National Awards

188. The enforcement of national arbitral awards is subject to the same rules as the enforcement of court judgments (*see* Part IX, Chapter 2.).

The enforcement of the award can be brought to a stop under a proposal from the obliged person due to the same reasons as a civil execution. The Act on Arbitration and the Enforcement of the Arbitral Awards regulates other reasons to halt the execution (the party is not obliged prior to ask the abolishment of the award by the court generally):

- if there is any defect of the award for which it could be abolished;
- if the party of the arbitration had to be represented by the legal representative, and there was a lack of this representation; and
- if the representative of the party was not entitled to represent.

The procedure consists of the suspension of the execution, and the obliged person is called up to propose the abolishment of the award by the court within a thirty-day time limit. If there is no such a proposal, the court of execution will continue the execution after the expiration of the time limit.

§2. Recognition and Enforcement of Foreign Awards

I. Rules Applicable in the Absence of a Treaty

189. If the legal relationship with a foreign is the subject of arbitration, the arbiters will decide the dispute under the law mutually chosen by the parties. The choice law or legal system relevant under the conflict rules is considered to be the substantive law, which would be chosen as relevant.

If the parties did not choose the law, the arbiters would consider the dispute under the law determined by the conflict rules.

The arbitration awards issued in the foreign State will be recognized and enforced if reciprocity is ensured. Reciprocity is also considered to be ensured if the foreign State declares the arbitration awards enforceable generally under reciprocity.

The decision on enforcement of the foreign arbitration award has to be reasoned. The recognition of the foreign arbitration award is not declared by the special decision. The foreign arbitration award is recognized in as much as it will be considered.

The recognition and the enforcement of the arbitration award will be refused if:

- the arbitration award is not in legal force or enforceable under the law of the country it was issued in;

– the arbitration award has any of defects which may cause the abolishment of the arbitration award by the court; and
– the arbitration award disaccords the public order.[13]

II. International Treaties

190. The international treaties on recognition and enforcement of foreign arbitration awards are either bilateral or multilateral.

The most relevant multilateral treaty is the New York UN Convention on the Recognition and Enforcement of Foreign Arbitration Awards of 10 June 1958 (published as No. 74/1959 Coll.). The other treaty is the multilateral Convention on Settlement of the Investment Disputes Between the States and the Citizens of the Another States of 1965 (Convention on the International Centre for Settlement of Investment Disputes – ICSID). The applicability of the European Convention on Arbitration of 1964 (the Geneva Convention on Arbitration No. 176/1964 Coll.) is limited, because of its narrow-mindedness as regards the parties involved due to the politics of the Cold War. The participants of the Convention are in addition simultaneously the parties of the New York Convention.

There is also the Inter-American Convention on International Commercial Arbitration. There are a large number of bilateral treaties concerned with the arbitration, especially conventions on promotion and protection of investment and on-air services and the like.

The Czech Republic is one of the Member States of the New York Convention. Under this Convention, the Member States are obliged to recognize the validity of arbitration agreements and to recognize and to enforce arbitration awards. The party asking for recognition and enforcement in a country which is party to the Convention has to connect its request to the original of the arbitration award and the original of the arbitration agreement (or its certified copies) with the official interpretation of the language of the State in which it will be recognized or enforced. The enforcement and recognition can be refused only due to reasons explicitly stated in the Convention (*see* Article V paragraph 1).

Consumer protection issues were excluded from the jurisdiction of the arbitrators by the law since December 2016.

13. A. Winterová, A. Macková et al., *Civilní právo procesní* (*The Civil Procedure Law*), II 2nd edn. (Leges Praha a.s. 2018), p. 30; T. Taylor & N. Cooper, *European Litigation Handbook* (London: Sweet and Maxwell, 1995).

Part XI. Mediation

Chapter 1. Legislation/Definitions

191. Mediation is a legal method of alternative dispute resolutions (ADR) as well as arbitration or consumer dispute resolution (by the Czech Commercial Inspection or Energetic Regulatory Authority, Czech Telecommunication Authority, Financial Arbiter or Ombudsman of the Czech Insurance Association – stipulated by the Consumer Protection Law – No. 634/1992 Coll. as amended). In the Czech Republic it has been regulated by the law since 1 September 2012.

The legal basis is the Act No. 202/2012 Coll. on Mediation and the Regulation of the Ministry of Justice No. 277/2012 Coll. On Exams and the Fee of the Mediators.

Mediation is the procedure for the settlement of the conflict with the participation of one or more mediators, who support the communication between the persons who are involved in the conflict, in order to help them achieve an amicable settlement of the conflict by the making of a mediation agreement.

For the conflict arising from family relations, there is a special family mediation.

A mediator is anyone who is registered in the special register of mediators (*see* – www.justice.cz).

Chapter 2. Rights That Can Be Subject to Mediation

192. Under Czech law, mediation is extensively admissible. The subject of the mediation agreement could be any private law rights and duties (e.g., commercial law matters, property law, family law, copyright and labour law,).

Fundamentally, the mediation is chosen by the parties voluntarily and consensually. However, the CPC stipulates conditions under which the meeting with mediator might be mandatory for the parties. If the court imposes mediation, it may include just the first meeting with a mediator (maximum three hours). The aim is to inform the parties about the relevancy and legal effects of mediation or its mere existence. Besides this general power to order a meeting with the mediator, the execution rules stipulate such an order if the obliged party does not respect the judgment on the custodial care on the minor.

Chapter 3. Mediation Agreement

193. The mediation agreement is the goal of the mediation by which the rights and duties of the parties are adjusted. It has to be signed by all the parties of the conflict. Its formal requirements are the signatures of the parties, the date of its making, refilled by the mediator and his/her signature, confirming that the mediation agreement was made as a result of the mediation.

The mediation agreement in itself is not enforceable, but the parties may ask the court to approve it as a consent decree or to ask notary to issue a notarial deed. After such a procedure at the court or at the notarial office, the mediation agreement may either be enforced by the court or by the (court) executor.

Chapter 4. Persons Who Can Act as Mediator

194. Mediation can be performed by the authorized persons only, i.e., the persons enrolled on the list of mediators (a public register at the Ministry of Justice, *see* www.justice.cz), as a mediator might be listed a person who is fully legally cap able, blameless and graduate in the master study programme, if the special exams of mediator were successfully passed. The exam might be passed either at the Min istry of Justice Commission or at the Czech Bar Commission (if the applicant is an attorney).

195. A visiting mediator can act and perform the mediation in the Czech Republic (if admitted as a mediator in the Member State of EU).

A mediator's liability covers the course of the mediation, but he/she is not liable for its result. The mediator has to be independent and impartial; in other case, he/she has to disclaim the mediation in the particular case (in the conflict of the interest or if the mutual confidence is disturbed). He/she has to act personally and with the proper professional care and has to keep the secrecy.

He/she acts for the fee, and he/she is entitled for his/her costs to be compensated. The agreement (contract on the mediation) between the parties and the mediator has to arrange the rule on the mediator's fee (and costs).

Chapter 5. Mediation Procedure

196. After the parties are instructed by the mediator on their rights and duties and the relevance and the effects of the mediation agreement, the contract between them and the mediator (the contract on the mediation) can be arranged and signed (its requisites are strictly stipulated by the law).

197. Then, the mediation's course is started (with the personal activity of the mediator, his/her keeping secrecy and with proper professional care). The proper performance of the mediation needs special skills (to listen, to respect the different views, to look for the conditions for the best solutions, to prefer the interests of the minor in the family mediation and many others) by which only it is possible to reach the goal of the mediation: to support the communication between the parties and to reach the settlement of their conflict.

198. The mediator has a duty to certify a mediation agreement of the parties and to confirm its existence. The course of the mediation in the particular case is governed by the rules, which are negotiated in the contract between the parties and the mediator (or it can refer to any special existing rules). The parties are thus bound by those rules, but still a general principle of the mediation, their voluntariness and the control over the mediation by the parties, must be followed. Special supportive rules on delivery in the course of the mediation and potential transfer of rights in the course of the mediation follow from the law.

Chapter 6. Settlement Agreement (A Mediation Agreement)

199. The mediation agreement is the intended goal of the mediation. Besides, the mediation may be through without this agreement and with any other solution of the conflict.

The mediation agreement is the written agreement between the parties of the conflict adjusting their rights and duties. The mediator is not the contractor of this agreement, but he/she has to certify its date and signing of the agreement by the parties, to issue his/her declaration on the mediation and to sign it.

The mediation agreement might be submitted by the parties to the court and approved as a consent decree upon their request. Without this approval, the mediation agreement is not admitted as the title for execution (it could not be enforced). The same applies if the parties ask the notary to issue a notarial deed on their mediation agreement.

Chapter 7. Setting Aside a Settlement Agreement

200. The settlement agreement adjusts the rights and duties of the parties. The principle of voluntariness governs the mediation as a matter of principle. From its nature thus follows that the parties may apply to the court to approve it as a consent decree or ask the notary to issue a notarial deed or they may surrender this. If there is no court or notarial approval, the settlement agreement has the same effects like any other agreement. It is not enforceable (the tittle for execution). The parties might always bring a lawsuit and ask the court to protect their rights.

201. The same applies when the mediation was not successful, i.e., if all parties deny the mediation or if the contract on mediation expired. The mediation will end also if:

(a) there is no interest of the parties in it (no meeting more than a year);
(b) the mediator is no longer convinced that the mediation could be successful; and
(c) the violation of the duty of the party to put down the deposit, which could be agreed upon in the mediation contract.

Chapter 8. International Mediation

202. The Directive No. 2008/52/ES was implemented fully in the Czech legal system. The Mediation – as a legally validated (legal) method of the alternative method of the disputes resolution – is widely admitted by the Czech law. The parties may thus agree on the mediation regardless of any limitation.

A mediation might be performed in the Czech Republic either by Czech Mediators (enrolled at the list at the Ministry of justice or the Czech Bar) or by the mediators, who are entitled to perform a mediation in any EU Member State. They will be listed after the certification of their permission to perform a mediation issued by the relevant authority in their country.

Selected Bibliography

Bílek, P., Drápal, L., Jindich, M., Wawerka, K., *Notáský ád a ízení o dědictví. (Notaries Rules and the Inheritance Proceedings on Herritage)*. C.H. Beck, 2018.

David, L., et al., *Civil Procedure Code, Commentary I. and II.* Wolters Kluwer, 2009.

Macková, A. *Česká advokacie a vstup České republiky do EU.* ('The Czech Bar and Access of the Czech Republic to EU') in *Czech Law in the EU*. Iuridica: Acta Universitatis Carolinae, 1-2/2004.

Macková, A. *Nezávislost soudc (The Independence of the Judge)*, 3rd edn. UK Praha, 1998.

Macková, A. Právní pomoc (historické ko eny a ešení), ('The Legal Aid – Historical Roots and Solutions'), in *The Recodification of the Private Law*. Iuridica: Acta Universitatis Carolinae, 1-2/2003.

Macková, A. *Právní pomoc advokát u a její dostupnost. (Attorneys and Their Services)*. C.H. Beck, 2001.

Taylor, T. & N. Cooper. *European Litigation Handbook*. London: Sweet and Maxwell, 1995.

Winterová A. *Žaloba v právu procesním (The Claim in Procedural Law)*. UK, Praha, 1979.

Winterová, A., Macková A., et al., *Civilní právo procesní I. and II (The Civil Procedure Law)*, 9th and 2nd edn. Leges Praha a.s., 2018.

Svejkovský, J., Vychope, M., Macková, A., et al., The Attorneys Law C.H.Beck, Prague, 2017

www.usoud.cz.

www.nsoud.cz.

www.nkcr.cz.

www.cak.cz.

www.ekcr.cz.

www.soud.cz.

www.soud.cz

www.jacz.cz

Selected Bibliography

Index

The numbers here refer to paragraph numbers.

Index

Index

Made in the USA
Monee, IL
18 October 2026

66041379R10070